BEST SALADS *ever*

BEST SALADS
ever

Sonja Bock & Tina Scheftelowitz

grub street | london

A THANK YOU TO YOU, DEAR READER

All the responses we receive are super inspiring. Thank you to Hanne Paludan, Gasa Nord Grønt and Yding Grønt A/S for finding new salads and descriptions for us.

This edition published in 2015 by
Grub Street
4 Rainham Close
London
SW11 6SS
Email: food@grubstreet.co.uk
Web: www.grubstreet.co.uk
Twitter: grub_street
Facebook: Grub Street Publishing

Copyright this English language edition © Grub Street 2015
Copyright © JP/Politikens Forlagshus København 2008
Translation by Anne Marie Tremlett
Design by Alette Bertelsen
Photos by Ditte Isager , Columbus Leth and Anders Schønnemann

A CIP record for this title is available from the British Library

ISBN 978-1-909808-33-1

Printed and bound in Malta

Contents

For readers who love superb salads 9
Special ingredients 11
Techniques 14
Tips and tricks 16

SUPERB SALADS
Beetroot salads 18
Cabbage salads 24
Root vegetable salads 36
Potato salads 44
Noodles, pasta, grain and seeds 52
Bean salads 64
The hit list 72
Green salads 74
Asparagus salads 86
Tomato salads 88
Salads with avocado, peppers, aubergine or pumpkin 92
Salads with fish 98
Salads with meat 104
Salads with fruit 108
Dips and salsas 114
Dressings, creams and pestos 124

BRILLIANT BUFFETS
Fish dishes for buffets 132
Meat dishes for buffets 140
Bread and cakes for buffets 147
Smaller buffets 154
Party buffets 160

Superb seasons 168
Index 170

TINA SCHEFTELOWITZ

SONJA BOCK

For readers who love superb salads

This book gives you a multitude of inspirational salads made with the best fresh ingredients.

We have set out to make every single salad an experience in itself, whether it is an unexpected combination of fresh ingredients, a new and exciting ingredient or just a wonderful flavour.

We have become brilliant at avoiding fat and oil and instead use sweet-sour-bitter-spicy ingredients for flavour. There are a lot of dressings which do not need oil, for example raw salads, salads with miso dressing and salads with seeds and nuts for topping. We have also used all the new ingredients which have come onto the market, or which we have recently discovered: Miso (Japanese fermented soya beans), wasabi (Japanese horseradish), quinoa (a type of South American 'grain') the good whole grain in the form of whole spelt, wholemeal and buckwheat pasta and many more.

We hope you will enjoy the book in big crunchy mouthfuls. Bon appetit!

SONJA

TINA

Special ingredients

Most of the fresh ingredients in this book are available either from your local greengrocer or from supermarkets. But for some ingredients you will need to go a little further. You will find these at Chinese grocers or greengrocers, in well stocked supermarkets, health food shops or delicatessens.

If you want to save time, call the shop first and ask if they have what you are looking for. And encourage them to stock it. You could also try the internet. There are several e-shops that sell spices and speciality foods.

GROUND SPICES Always remember to close the bags securely after use, and remember to discard the spices sometime after opening. An opened bag of curry powder that is 5 years old does not have much flavour. Think of the ground spices as ground coffee. They will not keep fresh for very long since the aromatic compounds are short lived and break down on contact with oxygen.

PEPPER Always used freshly ground pepper. A good quality pepper mill is indispensable.

GROUND ANISE Anise seeds look like fennel seeds and the taste is similar to star anise. Available as seed or ground from health food shops and Asian grocers.

DRIED HERBS After the bags have been opened the herbs will not keep fresh for very long.

CRUNCHY PEANUT BUTTER

TAHINI paste made from sesame seeds. Available from Asian grocers and supermarkets.

BALSAMIC VINEGAR Italian fermented vinegar available in many qualities, both red and white. We use a medium quality, i.e. not the cheapest, but not the most expensive one either, where each drop is worth gold.

OIL Use a medium olive oil for frying and a good super quality virgin olive oil for everything else. Have a taste of several different oils and experience the difference.

A good olive oil can make all the difference to your salad. It does not necessarily have to be the most expensive oil, but it is generally not the cheapest.

LEMON OLIVE OIL Available from Italian delicatessens and well stocked supermarkets. You can also make your own from good quality olive oil and lemon zest - it is just easier to buy the ready made one.

NEUTRAL TASTING OIL We use it especially for the Asian, Indian and South American salads and you could for

example use rape seed oil or corn oil.

DARK SESAME OIL Available from Asian grocers and well stocked supermarkets.

MISO is a fermented soya bean product which is a staple ingredient in Japanese cooking. It is very healthy, good for hangovers and an excellent flavour enhancer. There are many different types of miso. The light miso has the mildest flavour, the dark miso is stronger. In Japan, miso is available in many different qualities, but here we do not have quite the same choice. The dark miso is generally available from health food shops and some supermarkets, both kinds are usually available from Asian grocers.

QUINOA There is nothing negative to say about quinoa, the South American 'Golden Grain'. Quinoa is a gluten-free seed of the chenopodiaceae family of plants. It tastes wonderful, it is easy to use and it is super healthy. Use it hot instead of rice etc. And cold like bulgur in salads. If quinoa is part of your basic diet, you do not need to eat meat, unless of course you like the taste of meat. Quinoa is full of proteins, and on top of that has the perfect amino acid combination.

MUSCOVADO SUGAR

WHOLE SPELT, WHOLE GRAIN PASTA, BROWN BASMATI RICE, BUCKWHEAT NOODLES Forget about quick carbohydrates in white pasta and refined rice and choose instead whole grains and cereals with plenty of fibre. As well as the wonderful flavour,

you will also have plenty of fibres which are super healthy for your digestive system and help to prevent many illnesses. The fibres also help you feel full and will give you a healthy thirst so you automatically drink more water.

EDAMAME BEANS are green soya beans in their pod and they are often served as a snack in many Japanese restaurants. The flavour is fantastic. You don't eat the pod, only the beans, which you squeeze out of their pod with your teeth. For using in salads the beans are easily taken out of their pods with your fingers. Available frozen from Asian grocers.

SEAWEED Dried Japanese seaweed is available in many different qualities for example: Nori seaweed sheets, which are used for wrapping sushi rolls and as strips for garnishing; wakame seaweed, which is used in salads and soups, turns green when boiled: hijiki and arame seaweed which are used in salads. Seaweed is very healthy and rich in proteins, contains many minerals and vitamins and helps to lower cholesterol and blood pressure. It has the best flavour when marinated. Available from health food shops and Asian grocers.

JAPANESE SOY SAUCE is a world of its own. There are almost as many different types of soy sauce as there are wines in France. Every region has its own soy sauce and the quality varies enormously. The best known brand of soy sauce in this country is Kikkoman which is good for marinades and sauces, as it has a very strong flavour. Yamasa is lighter, less salty and less caramelised. Tamari which we have used in this book is a strong type which can be replaced with the milder variety. They are available from Asian supermarkets and health food shops.

WASABI is a Japanese horseradish which is pale green and very strong. Available as a paste in tubes, and as a powder which you mix with water to a suitable consistency. For the recipes in this book we have used the paste variety. It is used for sushi and as a flavour enhancer in several dishes, especially salads. All wasabis vary in strength so try different ones to find the one that suits you best.

COCONUT FLAKES are much better in salads than grated coconut, which you can of course use if you can't get hold of coconut flakes. Toast before use to

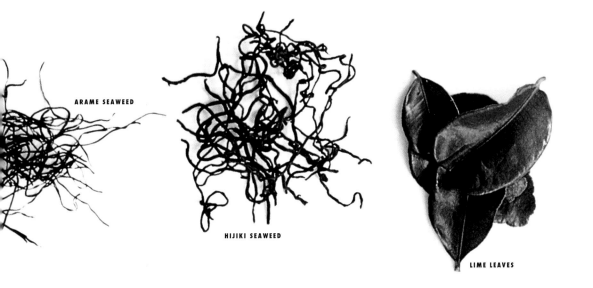

ARAME SEAWEED

HIJIKI SEAWEED

LIME LEAVES

develop the flavour. Available from health food shops and well stocked supermarkets.

GOOD SWEETENERS Muscovado sugar is unrefined cane sugar. Brown soft sugar can be used instead. Muscovado sugar is just more aromatic. Again: Taste the difference. Available from supermarkets and health food shops. If you use maple syrup, honey or muscovado sugar as a sweetener, it will give the salads an extra spicy kick. You can vary your own recipes by replacing sugar with one of these products.

YOGHURT Greek yoghurt with 10% fat is a wonderful sour milk product. Greek yoghurt with 0% fat has no flavour at all. We use crème fraîche with 9% fat if we want a thinner consistency and if the yoghurt taste does not suit the salad. Natural yoghurt with 3.5% fat (whole milk yoghurt) is also suitable for some dressings. It should preferably be organic. Look for organic dairy products from supermarkets and

health food shops.

FETA CHEESE Forget about feta cheese in cubes and low fat feta. Buy the genuine article from delicatessens or the best quality from supermarkets. Find the one you like best by tasting different ones.

NIGELLA SEEDS from the plant 'Love in the mist', are small black seeds. Traditionally used to sprinkle on top of bread like poppy seeds. Very good flavour enhancer in potato salads, root vegetable salads etc. Should always be toasted in a pan or baked to bring out the flavour.

LIME LEAVES Look like fresh bay leaves but taste of lime/lemon. Available both frozen and fresh from Asian grocers and well stocked supermarkets. Store in the deep freezer and take out as needed. Can be replaced by grated zest of lime but it is not quite the same. The dried ones available from supermarkets are not suitable for salads.

LEMON ZEST USING A CITRUS ZESTER

SALADS IN MOUTH-SIZE PIECES

Techniques

See also finely grated ginger page 29
and cutting citrus fillets page 80

FINELY CUT GARLIC

FINELY CUT LIME LEAVES

**ROOT VEGETABLES CUT INTO
JULIENNE STRIPS**

LEEKS CUT IN JULIENNE STRIPS

> Raw ingredients are given in unprepared quantities (unless otherwise indicated). Herbs are mainly stated in chopped quantity.

tips and tricks

> All recipes are tested and are for 4-6 people – depending on whether they are served as a main meal in themselves or as side dishes with fish or meat.

ABOUT THE BOOK All recipes are tested and are for 4-6 people depending on whether they are served separately as a meal in themselves or as side dishes with fish or meat. With fish or meat they could be served as one of several side dishes or just one side dish.

CLEANING All vegetables must of course be rinsed/washed/scrubbed if you want to avoid bacteria and grit in the food. To save space, we have chosen to mention this only for the lesser known vegetables, or if we know of some good tips for cleaning.

SALAD SPINNER Use for washing green salads. The best one is a plastic bowl with a plastic net inside and a lid with a handle for turning. Available in several sizes. You can dry salads without spilling water over the entire kitchen.

FRESH GREENS AND FRUIT Always use completely fresh vegetables and fruits, but make sure they are ripe, so the flavour and the aromatic compounds (the fruit sugars) are properly developed.

For example compare the juice of a hard yellow-green lemon with the juice of a soft, completely yellow and ripe lemon! There is a big difference. Use the juice of the lime fruit when it is soft and the colour of the peel begins to turn yellow. Use tomatoes that are ripened on the vine. A melon is ripe when it has an aroma on the outside, especially near the stalk.

QUANTITIES For quantities we have used proper measuring spoons. Please note that a tablespoon and a teaspoon from the cutlery drawer can vary enormously in size. It is therefore always a good idea to taste the food – both while you are preparing it and before serving. The extra minutes you spend on tasting makes the difference that gives the salad the last definitive kick, and you will be well rewarded.

Oven temperatures are indicated for hot air ovens. If you use an ordinary oven the temperature should be 25 degrees higher.

LARGE QUANTITIES If you are making large quantities of the individual salads, do not double the quantity of the dressings – the salad will be too wet, rather reduce accordingly.

SIMMERING To simmer means that you adjust the heat downward so the dish is kept at or just below boiling point. It is the exact opposite of fierce boiling.

FRESH HERBS We use a lot of fresh herbs in our book.
We believe they have a more exciting flavour than the dried ones. The best herbs are fresh herbs in bunches. Professional cooks buy them wholesale at the market, but the consumer often has to make do with the slightly boring pots of herbs from supermarkets and greengrocers. Therefore:
Ask your greengrocer to order fresh bunches of herbs.
Or grow your own.

CHILLI It is difficult to give the precise quantity for fresh chilli, the quantity is therefore always approximate in the recipes. We have used the medium sized chillies. The smaller the chillies, the hotter they are. Find the one you like best by tasting different ones.

GARLIC Should garlic be crushed or chopped? A good quality garlic press is more effective, if you are not very skilled with the kitchen knife. If garlic is chopped it must be very finely chopped. The onion taste will be a little stronger when you use a garlic press, but we believe that is absolutely fine. What you do is up to you and how you like it.

PASTA AND NOODLES If you rinse pasta and noodles in cold water after boiling and leave them to drain, they will not stick together.

GENERAL SALADS must be served as quickly as possible after preparation to make sure the ingredients remain fresh and crisp. But if you haven't got time to prepare the salad just before serving you should cover it well with cling film or foil and put it in a cool place. The dressing should be added only just before serving. And do not garnish salads until the last second before serving.
Salads should not be served directly from the fridge. If they have been prepared in advance they should be taken out of the fridge about 30 minutes before serving.

When you prepare buffets for lunch or parties it is of course practical to be able to prepare as much as possible in good time beforehand. For the buffets we have therefore indicated how soon the salads can be prepared in advance.

Beetroot salads

Beetroot can be used for much more than pickling. They are healthy, beautiful to look at and taste wonderful in salads whether raw or boiled.

BEETROOT WITH YOGHURT,
COFFEE AND WALNUTS, PAGE 23

BEETROOT WITH CRUNCHY
SALSA VERDE, PAGE 23

Beetroot in yoghurt with herbs

This salad has a simple, fresh flavour which makes it ideal for combining with other salads/ vegetables and for buffets. It goes well with most meat and fish.

900 g beetroot
100 ml Greek yoghurt with 10% fat
1 tbsp freshly squeezed lemon juice
5 tbsp finely chopped parsley
2 tbsp finely chopped mint
Salt and pepper

Boil the beetroot until tender, ½ - 1 hour depending on size. Pour over cold water and 'slip' them out of the skin. If necessary use a vegetable knife. Cut into cubes of approx. 1 x 1 cm, add yoghurt, lemon juice and half the herbs, and season to taste. Just before serving garnish with the remaining herbs on top.

**BEETROOT IN YOGHURT
WITH HERBS**

Beetroot salad with beetroot bruschetta

Have it for lunch or as an evening meal, for a buffet, or as a first course for 8 people. For the latter you could serve it with slices of Parma ham or bake the bruschetta with goat's cheese. Beetroot bruschettas are a hit. They can also be eaten as snacks without the salad, baked with a slice of goat's cheese on top. You can either bake the breads with the filling as in the recipe or add it 'raw' to the already baked bread.

400 g beetroot
1 (200 g) apple
2 tbsp balsamic vinegar
1 tbsp olive oil
1 handful chopped lovage
   (or basil)
Salt and pepper

BRUSCHETTA
4-8 slices (150 g)
   Italian bread
1 tbsp pine kernels
100 g beetroot
2 tbsp finely grated Parmesan
1 garlic clove, peeled and
   crushed
1 tbsp olive oil
Salt and pepper

Boil the beetroots until tender, ½ -1 hour depending on size. Pour over cold water and 'slip' them out of the skin. Cut the beetroots into thin slices. Cut the apple into quarters, remove and discard the core and slice the apple quarters thinly. Mix the beetroot slices, slices of apple, vinegar, oil, lovage, (save half for garnishing), salt and pepper and season the salad to taste.

BRUSCHETTA Toast the pine kernels until golden in a dry, hot pan. Chop roughly. Peel and grate the beetroot on the fine side of the vegetable grater. Mix the pine kernels, Parmesan, garlic, oil, beetroot, salt and pepper and season to taste. Put the bread slices on a baking tray lined with baking paper. Spoon 2 tsp of the mixture on to each slice of bread. Bake the bread in the oven at 175°C hot air/gas 6 for approx. 10 minutes until golden at the edge. Serve hot or lukewarm.

Beetroot with dill and lemon zest

1 kg beetroot
Zest of 1 organic lemon
3 tbsp olive oil
3 tbsp balsamic vinegar
1 tbsp finely chopped red
   salad onion (or ordinary
   onion)
5 tbsp chopped dill
Salt and pepper

Boil the beetroot until tender,
½-1 hour depending on size.
Pour over cold water and 'slip'
them out of the skin.
If necessary use a vegetable
knife. Cut into strips of
approx. 6 x 1 x ½ cm. Add the
other ingredients. Leave the
beetroots to cool, then add
the dill. Add salt and pepper
to taste.

**If you want to avoid
red fingers, wear
plastic gloves when
handling beetroot. Plastic
bags can be used,
if necessary.**

Baked beetroot with crunchy salsa verde

See photo page 18.

1.2 kg beetroot
4 tbsp olive oil
Salt and pepper
1 tbsp white wine vinegar
5 tbsp finely chopped parsley
5 tbsp finely chopped fresh
 basil (or tarragon)
2 tbsp chopped capers
2 garlic cloves, peeled and
 finely chopped

Peel the beetroots, and cut them into thin slices of approx. ½ cm. Line a baking tray with baking paper, mix the beetroot with oil, salt and pepper, and bake them in the oven at 175°C hot air/gas 6 for approx. 40 minutes.

Leave the beetroots to cool, mix in the other ingredients, and season to taste.

Beetroot with yoghurt, coffee and walnuts

See photo page 18. Beetroot and coffee sounds strange, but it tastes delicious.

900 g beetroot
70 g walnuts

COFFEE CREAM
100 ml Greek yoghurt
 with 10% fat
1 tbsp ground good quality
 coffee
2 tbsp freshly squeezed
 lemon juice
Salt and pepper

Boil the beetroot until tender, ½ -1 hour depending on size. Pour over cold water and 'slip' them out of their skin. If necessary use a vegetable knife. Cut them into smaller pieces, for example lengthways and then into slices.

Mix the coffee cream and leave it to settle while the beetroots are left to cool. Toast the nuts in a dry, hot pan until golden. Chop into smaller pieces. Add the cream to the beetroot and season to taste.
TO SERVE Garnish with the walnuts.

Baked beetroot with caraway seed and yoghurt

1.2 kg beetroot
3 tbsp olive oil
2 tsp whole caraway seeds
 (or cumin seeds)
200 ml natural yoghurt
Salt and pepper

Peel the beetroot, and cut them into wedges of approx. 6 x 1 cm. Line a baking tray with baking paper, mix the beetroot with oil, caraway seed, salt and pepper, and bake in the oven at 175°C hot air/gas 6 for approx. 50 minutes until baked through. Turn them a little during cooking. Leave the beetroots to cool, and then add the yoghurt and season to taste.

Cabbage salads

If you are looking for new ways of making the ever popular American coleslaw we have a few variations here. Coleslaw goes well with most dishes, but it is traditionally served as a side dish with grilled meat and baked potato. Try it with fish too. The original recipe contains mayonnaise, but we prefer Greek yoghurt with 10% fat which gives it the right fresh and rounded flavour. Cut the cabbage finely with a sharp knife or use the food processor for slicing it into very fine strips.

Red cabbage with fruit and toasted walnuts

This is a delicious and less fatty alternative to the Waldorf salad. A wonderful winter salad which is excellent with duck and any other dishes with which you would normally serve Waldorf salad.

300 g red cabbage
250 g celery
200 g seedless green grapes
100 g dry dates
50 g walnuts
150 g apple
3 tbsp freshly squeezed
    orange juice
Zest of ½ orange
1 tbsp clear honey
2 tsp apple cider vinegar
Salt and pepper

Remove any discoloured outer leaves, cut the cabbage in four, remove the stalk then slice the cabbage finely. Remove the top, bottom and the leaves from the celery and slice it finely. Cut the grapes into halves, or cut them into quarters if they are large. Remove the stones from the dates and cut the dates into smaller pieces. Toast the walnuts in a dry, hot pan and chop them. Remove the core and cut the apple into small cubes. Mix the ingredients for the dressing and pour it over the salad. Mix it all quickly and season to taste.

Asian green cabbage salad

Green cabbage is super healthy and cheap and is brilliant for every day cooking during the winter period. A few variations are therefore welcome and the following recipes will give you just that. This is an Asian inspired salad which is excellent with Asian dishes or any kind of neutral meat or fish that need a bit of a kick. You can use mixed fruit juice, pineapple juice or some of the good 'freshly squeezed' juices from supermarkets. Add fish sauce or Soy sauce instead of salt to taste.

150 g green cabbage
½ small (450 g) pineapple
½ red chilli (or to taste)
40 g toasted, salted peanuts
  (or cashew nuts)

DRESSING
100 ml exotic fruit juice
1 tbsp freshly squeezed
  lime juice
½ tbsp clear honey
1 tsp peeled, freshly
  grated ginger
Salt

Rinse the cabbage in several lots of water and use the salad spinner to dry it.

Cut the cabbage finely with a sharp knife. The finer, the better, otherwise the cabbage will tickle the roof of your mouth. It is easier to cut if you keep the stalk on the cabbage and then cut towards the stalk which you then discard. Cut the peel off the pineapple, cut thin slices of the fruit towards the centre all the way round the core which you then discard. Cut the slices into small cubes. Remove the seeds and membranes from the chilli and cut it into tiny cubes. Chop the peanuts roughly. Mix with the green cabbage, pineapple and chilli. Mix the dressing, go easy on the salt because of the peanuts, mix the dressing with the salad and season to taste.
TO SERVE Garnish with peanuts.

Summer slaw

Only make this salad when
the vegetables are in their
peak season during June-July.

350 g white summer cabbage
200 g new carrots
400 g peas in their pods

CREAM

200 g Greek yoghurt
    with 10% fat
1 tsp freshly squeezed
    lemon juice
3 tbsp chopped dill
3 tbsp finely chopped chives
1 tsp sugar
Salt and pepper

Remove the stalk of the white
cabbage and cut the cabbage
finely. Scrape and grate the
carrots. Pod the peas. Mix the
cream, add the vegetables and
season the salad to taste.

Mexi-slaw

Anise seeds look like fennel
seeds but taste a bit like star
anise. Available as seeds or
ground anise seed from health
food shops or Asian grocers.

350 g white cabbage
50 g green beans
250 g cherry tomatoes

CREAM

200 g Greek yoghurt
    with 10% fat
2 tsp finely chopped Jalapeños
    chilli (available sliced
    in jars)
1 tsp freshly squeezcd
    lemon juice
1 garlic clove, peeled and
    finely chopped
½ tsp ground anise seed
½ tsp ground coriander
1 tsp sugar
Salt

Remove the stalk from the
white cabbage and cut the
cabbage very finely. Trim the
beans and steam in a saucepan
under a lid in lightly salted
water, until almost tender,
approx. 3 minutes. Rinse
immediately in cold water.
Cut in halves crossways.
Cut the cherry tomatoes into
quarters and leave to drain in
a sieve. Mix the cream, add
the vegetables and season the
salad to taste.

Crisp vegetables in red curry cream

See photo page 31.
Coconut flakes are available from health food shops or well stocked supermarkets. The Thai curry paste is available from most major supermarkets or from Asian grocers.

100 g leeks
100 g carrots
250 g white cabbage
100 g sugar snaps
   (or a total of 550 g
   vegetables of your own
   choice)
20 g (1 handful) coconut
   flakes (or grated coconut)

1/2-1 tsp Thai red curry paste
200 ml crème fraîche, 9% fat
1 tbsp freshly squeezed
   lime juice (or lemon juice)
Salt

Cut the leeks into julienne strips, pour boiling water over and leave for a couple of minutes. Leave to drain in a sieve. Cut the carrots into julienne strips, cut the white cabbage finely and cut the sugar snaps into strips diagonally. Toast the coconut flakes in a dry, medium hot pan. Take care they don't turn dark, they should be golden.

Put the red curry paste in a bowl, add crème fraîche a little at a time then add salt and lime juice.

TO SERVE Mix the vegetables, curry cream and half the coconut flakes and season to taste. Sprinkle the rest of the flakes over the salad.

FINELY GRATED FRESH GINGER

Cabbage salad with seaweed & sesame oil

Seaweed and dark sesame oil are available from health food shops and Chinese grocers. Sesame oil is a fabulously delicious ingredient which really brings out the flavours.

10 g (1 handful) dried
   seaweed (Hijiki or Arame)
500 g white cabbage
   (or red cabbage)
200 g leeks
300 g apples
2 tbsp neutral tasting oil
1 tsp dark sesame oil
1 tbsp finely grated
   fresh ginger
4 tsp freshly squeezed
   lemon juice
Salt and pepper

Pour boiling water over the seaweed and leave to infuse for approx. 15 minutes, then drain off the water and discard. Remove the stalk from the white cabbage and cut the cabbage finely. Cut the leeks into julienne strips, rinse thoroughly in several lots of clean water, pour boiling water over and set aside for approx. 1 minute. Drain off the water. Cut the apples into julienne strips or thin wedges, do not peel the apples. Mix the vegetables and the dressing and season the salad to taste.

Arabic slaw

Tahini is a paste made from sesame seeds. Available from Asian grocers. The creamy dressing in this recipe can also be served as a cold sauce with all kinds of fish and meat.

350 g white cabbage
200 g carrots
5 tbsp finely chopped parsley

CREAM
3 tbsp tahini
1 garlic clove, peeled and
   finely chopped
200 ml natural yoghurt
1 tsp freshly squeezed
   lemon juice
Salt and pepper

Remove the stalk from the white cabbage and cut the cabbage very finely. Grate the carrots on the coarse side of the vegetable grater. Mix the cream, add the vegetables and parsley and season the salad to taste.

Red cabbage slaw with beetroot and tarragon cream

350 g red cabbage
200 g beetroot

200 g Greek yoghurt
   with 10% fat
1 tsp grated onion
2 tsp Dijon mustard
1 tsp sugar
2 tbsp chopped fresh tarragon
   (or 2 tsp dried)
1 tsp freshly squeezed
   lemon juice
Salt and pepper

Remove the stalk from the red cabbage and cut the cabbage very finely. Peel and grate the beetroot. Mix the cream and add the vegetables. Season to taste.

Coleslaw with pineapple and nuts

350 g white cabbage
400 g pineapple
30 g (3 tbsp) hazelnuts

CREAM
200 g Greek yoghurt 10% fat
1 tsp freshly squeezed
    lemon juice
1 tsp grated onion
1 tsp Dijon mustard
1 tsp sugar
Salt and pepper

Remove the stalk from the white cabbage and cut the cabbage very finely. Remove the peel and cut the pineapple into small cubes. Chop the nuts roughly and toast them in a dry, hot pan. Mix the cream, add the cabbage and pineapple and season to taste.
TO SERVE Mix in half the nuts and use the rest for garnishing.

Spring slaw

This salad should be made only when the vegetables are in their peak season during May-August.

300 g pointed cabbage
1 bunch radishes
200 g cucumber

150 g Greek yoghurt 10% fat
1 tbsp milk
1 tsp freshly squeezed
    lemon juice
4 tbsp finely chopped chives
1 tsp sugar
Salt and pepper

Remove the stalk from the pointed cabbage and slice the cabbage finely. Cut the radishes into thin slices. Cut the cucumber lengthways, scrape out the seeds with a teaspoon and cut into small cubes. Mix the cream, add the vegetables and season to taste.

Brussels sprouts with clementines and dates with nut-mint salsa

This salad tastes delicious with duck and roast pork, meatballs and poultry. The fresh mint used in this recipe is the Moroccan crispy mint which tastes delicious. The mint you buy in small pots is usually peppermint which has a different flavour. Order Moroccan mint from your greengrocer or buy it fresh in packets from well stocked supermarkets.

500 g Brussels sprouts
6 (500 g) clementines
1 small handful (50 g) dates
½-1 red chilli
½ handful fresh mint leaves

SALSA

50 g hazelnuts
½ handful fresh mint leaves
2 tbsp olive oil
2½ tbsp freshly squeezed
    lemon juice
Salt

Cut the stalk from the Brussels sprouts and remove the outer discoloured leaves. Cook the Brussels sprouts in a tightly covered pan with boiling salted water for approx. 5 minutes until almost tender. Rinse in cold water in a sieve, leave to drain and cool and cut into halves. Peel and cut the clementines in thin slices. Cut the dates into thin slices.

Remove the seeds and membranes from the chilli and cut into strips or chop finely.

SALSA Toast the nuts in a dry, hot pan, shake the pan all the time, until the skin loosens. Place the nuts on a clean tea towel and rub off the skin with the tea towel. Chop the nuts finely with a knife. Chop the mint finely. Mix nuts, mint, oil and lemon juice and add salt to taste. Marinade the cabbage in the salsa.

TO SERVE Chop the rest of the mint. Arrange cabbage and clementines on a serving dish, garnish with dates, chilli and mint.

Brussels sprouts with caramelised pistachio nuts

A very simple salad which goes with any meat or fish dish.

1 kg Brussels sprouts
100 g salted pistachio nuts in their shell
2 tsp honey

DRESSING
2 tbsp olive oil
2 tbsp balsamic vinegar
Salt and pepper

Cut the stalk from the Brussels sprouts and remove the outer discoloured leaves. Cook the Brussels sprouts in a tightly covered pan with boiling salted water for approx. 5 minutes until almost tender. Rinse under cold water in a sieve, leave the Brussels sprouts to drain and cool. Cut the Brussels sprouts into halves and mix in the dressing. Shell and roast the pistachio nuts in a dry, hot pan, add the honey and continue to stir until the honey has melted. Leave the nuts to cool on a plate.
TO SERVE Mix in the nuts and season to taste.

Brussels sprouts with red salad onion and feta cheese

Buy the best quality feta cheese you can get hold of.

1 kg Brussels sprouts
50 g red salad onion
75 g feta cheese
2 tbsp olive oil
4 tsp white balsamic vinegar
Salt and pepper

Cut the stalk from the Brussels sprouts and remove the outer discoloured leaves. Cook the Brussels sprouts in a tightly covered pan with boiling salted water until almost tender, approx. 5 minutes. Rinse under cold water in a sieve and leave to drain and cool. Cut the Brussels sprouts into halves or slice them. Chop the red salad onion finely and mix the dressing with the onion and Brussels sprouts. Crumble the feta over the vegetables and turn over carefully. Go easy on the salt since the feta cheese is salty.

Salad à la Christmas Eve

A must for the Christmas lunch table or bring it along for the December pot luck supper. A healthier, fresher and more exciting version of the traditional roast duck.

1 duck breast
2 tbsp roughly chopped thyme
1 tbsp neutral tasting oil for frying
300 g red cabbage
2 (300 g) apples
2 tbsp apple vinegar
Approx. 6 tsp redcurrant jelly
Salt and pepper

Remove the fat from the duck breast and cut the breast into small cubes. Cut the breast into slices of 1 cm. Fry the fat in a pan at medium heat, until the cubes are golden and crisp. Add thyme for the last few minutes. Turn over regularly; leave to drain on kitchen towel. Fry the duck breast slices in oil at high temperature for approx. 5 minutes in total, turn over once during cooking.
   Slice the cabbage finely with a sharp knife. Cut off the stalk and discoloured leaves and discard. Cut the apples into small cubes, cut away the apple core and discard. Mix the apple cubes in 1 tbsp vinegar. Mix cabbage, 1 tbsp vinegar, salt and pepper and season to taste. Arrange the cabbage on a serving dish.
TO SERVE Arrange the slices of duck on top of the cabbage, then the apples on top of the duck. Garnish with redcurrant jelly and 'duck crackling'.

Root vegetable salads

Root vegetables are healthy and taste delicious in a salad. Celeriac in particular is an underrated, but tasty, sweet vegetable which deserves to be much more widely used. The salads can be made in plenty of time before serving. You can cut the root vegetables into any shape you like, only adjust the cooking time accordingly. When the recipe says 'mixed root vegetables' you can use one or several kinds of root vegetables according to taste and availability.

Italian salad our way

It was not our intention to come up with an alternative Italian salad – it just ended up looking like the original. Make it when peas are in season. It is delicious with boiled ham, baked ham or poultry.

1 kg carrots
1 tbsp olive oil
Salt and pepper

PEA CREAM
300 g peas in their pod
200 ml natural yoghurt
1 garlic clove, peeled
   and finely chopped
5 tbsp finely chopped parsley
Salt and pepper

Cut the carrots into strips of approx. ½ x 1 x 7 cm. Mix with oil, salt and pepper and bake in an ovenproof dish lined with baking paper at 175°C hot air/gas 6 for approx. 45 minutes, until golden and tender. Turn over a few times during cooking. Leave the carrots to cool, mix the dressing and add to the carrots. Season to taste.

Baked carrots with
3 kinds of seed

Tastes delicious with
poultry and pork.

1.2 kg carrots
2 tbsp olive oil
2 garlic cloves, peeled
    and chopped
1 tsp fennel seed
1 tsp cumin seeds
½ tsp caraway seeds
1 pinch cayenne pepper
Salt
2 tbsp freshly squeezed
    lemon juice

Cut the carrots into strips
of approx. ½ x 1 x 7 cm.
Mix with oil, garlic and spices
and bake in an ovenproof dish
lined with baking paper at
175°C hot air/gas 6 for approx.
45 minutes, until golden and
tender. Turn over a few times
during cooking. Add lemon
juice and season to taste.

Baked carrots with
cumin and honey

1.2 kg carrots
2 tbsp olive oil
1 tbsp ground cumin
2 tsp clear honey
Salt and pepper
2 tbsp freshly squeezed
    lemon juice
TO GARNISH Finely chopped
    parsley.

Follow the recipe above.

Baked Hamburg parsley
with clementines and linseed

A delicious winter salad which is perfect with Christmas
dishes such as poultry and pork, but it also goes well with
lamb. Fresh mint is delicious for garnishing and flavour.

700 g Hamburg parsley
    or parsnips
1 tbsp olive oil
2 tbsp freshly squeezed
    lemon juice
5 (400 g) clementines
    (or equal quantity
    of oranges)
1 small handful (50 g) dried
    apricots
½-1 fresh red chilli
1 tbsp linseeds
Salt

Peel and cut the roots into
thin slices, mix with oil and
salt and place on a baking
tray lined with baking paper.
Bake in the oven at 200°C hot
air/gas 7 for approx. 20
minutes, until golden and
tender. Leave to cool and
mix with the lemon juice.
Peel the clementines, keep
them whole and cut into ten
thin slices. Cut the apricots
into thin slices.

Cut the chilli in half,
remove the seeds and
membranes and cut the chilli
into thin slices or chop finely.
Toast the linseeds in a dry, hot
pan while stirring all the time
until they pop. Remove from
the pan immediately.

TO SERVE Mix the baked roots,
clementines, apricots and
chilli. Sprinkle with a little
salt and garnish with the
linseeds.

BAKED HAMBURG PARSLEY WITH CLE-
MENTINES AND LINSEED

Sautéed summer turnip with cranberries and feta

The turnip is not used very often in cooking. This is a pity since the light bitterness gives an exciting dimension to salads. Young summer turnips are in season during May until July with the peak season in June.

The cranberries can be replaced with 50 g fresh blackcurrants.

500 g turnips
1 tbsp olive oil
1 tbsp balsamic vinegar,
    red or white + a little more
50 g rocket (or baby spinach)
8 tsp small feta cubes
2 tbsp dried cranberries
Salt and pepper

Cut the top and bottom of the turnips and cut into wedges of approx. 1½ cm. Pour the oil into a hot pan and fry the wedges at medium heat, sprinkle with salt and pepper, turn during cooking and fry for approx. 10 minutes, until golden and lightly crisp.

Leave to cool, then mix in the vinegar and season to taste. Rinse and dry the rocket, arrange on a serving dish.

TO SERVE Drizzle a little vinegar over the salad, place the turnip wedges on top, then small cubes of feta and finally the cranberries.

Baked celeriac with tapenade

Tapenade is a French dish consisting of puréed olives. The salad is delicious with poultry and lean fish.

1½ kg celeriac
2 tbsp olive oil
Salt and pepper

TAPENADE
50 g black olives, stone out
1 tbsp capers
1-2 garlic cloves, peeled
1 tbsp freshly squeezed
   lemon juice
Pepper

Cut the celeriac in strips of approx. ½ x 3 x 5 cm. Line a baking tray with baking paper, mix the celeriac with oil, a little salt and pepper. Bake at 175°C hot air/gas 6 for approx. ½ hour, until the strips are golden. Turn over a few times during cooking. Put all the ingredients for the tapenade in a food processor (or chop them finely with a sharp knife), mix with the celeriac and season to taste.

Baked carrots with ras el hanout

Ras el hanout means 'head of the shop' and it is a Moroccan spice mixture which comes in as many different variations as there are shops in the bazaar. The mixture has a wonderful flavour full of mystique and the long list of ingredients is worth all the trouble.

We have made a slightly bigger portion than the one needed for the salad. The mixture should be stored in an airtight container, and it is delicious with baked potato wedges, in meatballs and as a marinade for grilling etc. The salad goes well with all kinds of strong meat dishes, for example beef, lamb, venison, pork and oily fish.

1.2 kg carrots
2 tbsp olive oil
2 tbsp ras el hanout
Salt
2 tbsp freshly squeezed
   lemon juice

RAS EL HANOUT
4 bay leaves, rubbed into
   small bits
1 tbsp ground cinnamon
1 tbsp ground coriander
1 tbsp ground cumin
1 tbsp ground ginger
1 tbsp dried thyme
1 tsp grated nutmeg
½ tsp cayenne pepper
½ tsp ground anise seed
½ tsp ground cardamom
½ tsp ground cloves

Cut the carrots into strips of approx. ½ x 1 x 7 cm. Mix all the ingredients for the ras el hanout. Mix the carrots with oil, salt and ras el hanout and bake in an ovenproof dish lined with baking paper at 175°C hot air/gas 6 for approx. 45 minutes, until golden and tender. Turn over a few times during cooking. Add lemon juice and season to taste.

Baked celeriac with gremolata

Gremolata is traditionally the green topping used for osso bucco. You can substitute the parsley with mint and the lemon zest with the zest of an orange. Absolutely delicious.

1½ kg celeriac
2 tbsp olive oil
4 tsp freshly squeezed
 lemon juice
Salt and pepper

GREMOLATA
2 handfuls chopped parsley
2 garlic cloves, peeled and
 finely chopped
2 tsp finely grated zest of an
 organic lemon

Cut the celeriac into strips of approx. ½ x 1 x 7 cm. Line a baking tray with baking paper, mix the celeriac with oil, a little salt and pepper. Bake at 175°C hot air/gas 6 for approx. ½ hour, until the strips are golden. Turn over a few times during cooking. Mix in the lemon juice when the strips have cooled a little. Mix the gremolata with the salad and season to taste. It is easier to chop the garlic finely if you chop them together with the parsley.

Baked root vegetables with thyme and garlic mayonnaise

1½ kg mixed root vegetables,
 for example celeriac,
 Hamburg parsley, parsnip
 and carrots
½ pot freshly chopped thyme
 (or 1 tbsp dried)
1 tbsp olive oil
Salt and pepper

GARLIC MAYONNAISE
2 tbsp pasteurised egg yolk
2 tsp lemon juice
1 tsp Dijon mustard
2 garlic cloves, peeled and
 finely chopped
Approx. 6 tbsp neutral
 tasting oil
Approx. 1 tbsp water
Salt and pepper

Cut the root vegetables in strips of approx. ½ x 1 x 7 cm. Mix with oil, thyme, salt and pepper. Bake in a baking tray lined with baking paper at 175°C hot air/gas 6 for approx. 45 minutes, until golden and tender. Turn over a few times during cooking.

GARLIC MAYONNAISE Whisk the egg yolk with an electric hand whisk with lemon juice, mustard, garlic, salt and pepper. Mix in the oil – a little at a time – until the consistency is thick and creamy. Whisk in the water until the consistency is like crème fraîche 18%.

TO SERVE Arrange the root vegetables on a serving dish and spoon over the mayonnaise in a decorative pattern.

Baked root vegetables with poppy seeds

Poppy seeds can be used for many more dishes other than as a topping for bread. The flavour is deliciously piquant, if the seeds are baked to fully develop the flavour. Try also sprinkling a thick layer of poppy seeds on oven baked potato wedges or chicken. First coat the chicken with Dijon mustard to ensure the seeds will stick.

1½ kg mixed root vegetables,
 for example celeriac,
 Hamburg parsley, parsnips
 and carrots
2 tbsp olive oil
2 garlic cloves, peeled and
 finely chopped
2 tbsp blue poppy seeds
Salt and pepper
1½ tbsp balsamic vinegar
Finely chopped parsley

Cut the root vegetables into strips of approx. ½ x 1 x 7 cm. Mix with oil, garlic, salt and pepper. Sprinkle with poppy seeds and bake in a baking tray lined with baking paper at 175°C hot air/gas 6 for approx. 45 minutes, until golden and tender. Turn over a few times during cooking. Add vinegar to taste and sprinkle with chopped parsley.

Potato salads

Potatoes and beetroot in horseradish cream

Renew the great classic, 'Breast of beef in horseradish sauce' and serve this salad with the boiled breast of beef or with other cuts of boiled beef, for example stewing beef.

700 g small potatoes
300 g beetroot
100 g leeks
300 ml crème fraîche
   with 9% fat
3 tbsp whole, finely grated
   horseradish
4 tbsp white wine vinegar
1 tbsp sugar
Salt and pepper

Boil the potatoes, peel and leave them to cool, then cut into small cubes. Peel the beetroot, and cut them into cubes of approx. 1 x 1 cm. Boil in water for approx. 30 minutes until tender. Leave to cool. Cut the leeks into julienne strips, rinse thoroughly in several lots of clean water, then pour boiling water over the leeks and set aside for approx. 1 minute. Drain off the water. Mix the horseradish cream and add the potatoes, beetroot and half the leeks. Season to taste. Arrange in a serving bowl or dish and garnish with the rest of the leeks.

Small firm potatoes are the most suitable for salads, use new potatoes when in season. The small potatoes are also suitable for baking, alternatively use large baking potatoes cut into strips.

Potatoes with zhug

Zhug is a Yemenite chilli sauce. It is traditionally very hot, but you can adjust the strength according to your own taste by adding or leaving out (some of) the chilli. If the chilli is very mild the chopped seeds can be included or you can add more chillies.

1 kg small potatoes

ZHUG
1 green chilli
1 large pot/bunch of fresh
   coriander
100 ml olive oil
5 tsp freshly squeezed
   lemon juice
2 garlic cloves, peeled
½ tsp cumin seeds
½ tsp ground cardamom
Salt and pepper

Boil the potatoes, peel them and leave to cool, then cut into small cubes. Cut the chilli lengthways, remove the seeds and chop the chilli into small pieces. Chop the garlic. Blend all the ingredients for the zhug in a blender or food processor. Mix the potatoes with the dressing and leave the salad to rest for a minimum of ½ hour. Season to taste.

Potatoes with horseradish and lemon oil

1 kg small potatoes
3 tbsp lemon olive oil
   (or 2 tsp finely grated zest
   of a lemon and 3 tbsp
   olive oil)
1 tbsp freshly squeezed
   lemon juice
3 tbsp whole, fresh, finely
   grated horseradish
6 tbsp chopped parsley
Salt and pepper

Boil the potatoes, peel them and leave to cool, then cut into small cubes. Mix with the other ingredients and leave the salad to rest for at least ½ hour.
   Season to taste.

Potatoes in spring

Instead of the chicken breasts you could use 350 g potatoes to make the salad a vegetarian dish. You could also then serve it with for example pot roast chicken.

500 g small new potatoes
½ bunch rhubarb
2 tbsp sugar
2 chicken breasts,
   approx. 300 g
1 tbsp olive oil
100 g cucumber
Salt and pepper

RHUBARB CREAM
300 ml crème fraîche with
   9% fat
2 handfuls chopped parsley
   (or dill, lovage or chervil)
Juice from the rhubarb

Boil the potatoes, peel them and leave to cool, then cut into small cubes. Remove the leaves from the rhubarb and chop off any brownish bits at the opposite end. Cut the stalks into pieces of approx. 5 cm. Bake in a baking tray sprinkled with sugar at 175°C hot air/gas 6 for approx. ½ hour, until they are tender. The juice is also used. Cut the chicken breast into strips of approx. 1½ cm and fry in oil with salt and pepper at high temperature for approx. 4 minutes until cooked through. Leave to cool.
   Mix the cream (save a little parsley for garnishing) and add the chicken and potatoes. Cut the cucumber lengthways, remove the seeds with a teaspoon and cut crossways into thin slices.
   TO SERVE Arrange the salad on a serving dish and garnish with cucumber, rhubarb and parsley.

Potatoes and aubergines in tahini cream

Tahini is a paste made from sesame seeds. It is available from Asian grocers and typically used in hummus.

700 g small potatoes
350 g aubergines
2 tbsp olive oil
1 tbsp sesame seeds
Chopped parsley to garnish

TAHINI CREAM
2 tbsp tahini
200 ml natural yoghurt
1½ tbsp freshly squeezed
  lemon juice
1 garlic clove finely chopped
1 pinch cayenne pepper
Salt

Cut the aubergines into cubes of approx. 1½ x 1½ cm mix with oil, salt and pepper and bake in a baking tray lined with baking paper at 175°C hot air/gas 6 for approx. ½ hour until golden (not burnt) and tender. Turn over a few times during cooking. Boil the potatoes, peel and leave them to cool, then cut into small cubes. Toast the sesame seeds in a dry, hot pan until golden.

Mix the cream, add the potatoes and half the aubergines. Arrange on a serving dish and garnish with the rest of the aubergines, sesame seeds and parsley.

VARIATION
Potatoes and olives in tahini cream

1 kg potatoes, 150 g Kalamata olives stone in, the above cream and chopped broad leaved parsley for garnishing. Stone the olives and chop them roughly. Mix the sliced, boiled, peeled potatoes with the cream and two thirds of the olives, season to taste. Arrange in a serving bowl. Garnish with the rest of the olives and the parsley.

Baked potatoes with herbs and lemon

A neutral salad which is suitable for buffets, as it goes well with many different dishes. The herbs can be varied according to the dish with which you want to serve the potatoes.

1.2 kg small potatoes with the
  peel left on
2 tbsp olive oil
2 tbsp freshly squeezed
  lemon juice
3 handfuls chopped mixed
  herbs, for example thyme,
  parsley, tarragon, lovage,
  mint
Salt and pepper

Scrub the potatoes and mix them with oil, salt and pepper and bake with the peel left on in a baking tray at 225°C hot air/gas 9 for approx. 30 minutes, until golden and tender. Turn them over several times during cooking.Leave to cool, mix with lemon juice and herbs and season to taste.

Potato salad with mushrooms, spinach and miso dressing

Goes well with beef, poultry and fish. Read about the healthy and tasty miso on page 11 and the Japanese horseradish wasabi on page 12.

600 g potatoes
100 g baby spinach
150 g oyster mushrooms
(or other mushrooms)
1 tbsp neutral tasting oil
   for frying
Salt

MISO DRESSING

3 tbsp miso, light or dark
2 tsp peeled, finely grated
   fresh ginger
1 garlic clove, peeled
   and crushed
Approx. 1 tsp wasabi from
   a tube
1 tbsp apple cider vinegar
3 tbsp water

Scrub the potatoes and boil in lightly salted water in a saucepan with a tightly fitting lid until tender. Peel the potatoes, if necessary. Cut into slices/halves. Rinse the spinach in several lots of clean water, leave to drain and dry. Cut the mushrooms into strips and fry in a pan in the oil at medium temperature while continually stirring for approx. 15 minutes until golden.

Add half the spinach, remove the pan from the heat, stir the spinach until it wilts.
DRESSING Mix miso, ginger, garlic, wasabi, vinegar and water and season the dressing to taste.
TO SERVE Mix potatoes, mushrooms and spinach and arrange on a serving dish, drizzle the dressing over the salad.

Potatoes with rocket, lemon oil and pine kernels

Go hunting for the fantastic lemon olive oil in a well stocked supermarket or Italian delicatessen. Potatoes and lemon olive oil taste wonderful together.

900 g small potatoes
30 g (3 tbsp) pine kernels
100 g rocket
2 tbsp lemon olive oil
   (or 1 tsp finely grated
   zest of a lemon and 2 tbsp
   olive oil)
1 ½ tbsp freshly squeezed
   lemon juice
Salt and pepper

Boil the potatoes, peel them and leave to cool, then cut into small pieces. Toast the pine kernels in a dry, hot pan until golden. Remove the coarse stalks from the rocket and tear into smaller pieces. Mix the potatoes with all the ingredients except for the pine kernels and the rocket. Set aside.

TO SERVE Mix in the rocket and pine kernels and season to taste.

Indian inspired potato salad

Garam masala is a spice mixture similar to curry powder. Available from Asian grocers and supermarkets. The salad can be prepared with or without yoghurt. The cashew nuts are available toasted from most supermarkets.

700 g small potatoes
500 g cauliflower
1 ½ tbsp Garam masala
   (or curry powder)
3 tbsp neutral tasting oil
125 g cherry tomatoes
300 g fresh peas in their pod
1 ½ tbsp freshly squeezed
   lemon juice
100 ml natural yoghurt
   (or 1 extra tbsp lemon juice,
   if necessary)
40 g toasted cashew nuts
Salt and pepper

Cut the cauliflower into small florets of approx. 3 x 4 cm. Scrub the potatoes, leave the peel on, cut them in half, mix with oil, Garam masala and salt and bake with the cauliflower in a baking tray lined with baking paper at 225°C hot air/gas 9 for approx. 20 minutes, until golden and tender. Turn the vegetables over several times during cooking.

   Cut the cherry tomatoes in half and pod the peas. Mix yoghurt and lemon juice with the potatoes.

TO SERVE Mix the tomatoes, peas and, if necessary, chopped nuts and season the salad to taste.

Potato salad with nigella seeds and lemon dressing

Goes well with most meat and fish dishes. Read about nigella seeds on page 13.

800 g small potatoes
1 small (200 g) Romaine
   lettuce
1 tbsp nigella seeds
1 organic lemon
2-3 tbsp lemon olive oil
   (or olive oil and zest of
   1 extra lemon)
Salt and pepper

Scrub the potatoes and boil them in salted water in a saucepan with tightly fitted lid until tender. Peel the potatoes, if necessary. Cut into slices/halves. Slice the salad into strips and rinse in several lots of clean water, leave to drain and thoroughly dry. Toast the nigella seeds in a dry, hot pan until they give off an aroma, stirring all the time. Cut the zest of the lemon with a lemon zester or grate it finely on a vegetable grater, cover and set aside for garnishing. Remove the white membrane from the lemon and cut the lemon into thin slices.

   Mix the potatoes with half the seeds, the oil, the lemon slices and salt and season to taste.

TO SERVE Arrange the salad on a serving dish, and place the potatoes on top. Garnish with nigella seeds.

POTATO SALAD WITH NIGELLA SEEDS AND
LEMON DRESSING

Noodles, pasta, grain and seeds

Some people have the idea that pasta salad is one of the mistakes of the eighties. And the Italians would never dream of serving cold pasta. The idea originates, of course – like so many other things – from the USA. Nevertheless, in our experience many people love this type of salad. We therefore say: 'Give people what they like'. Noodle salads, on the contrary, are traditional in the Far East. In this book we are not making the classic recipes, but in our salads we use the region's raw materials in our own way. Try also whole spelt and quinoa in salads: It is healthy foundation food which tastes delicious. Noodle salads, like pasta salads, should contain at least 50% vegetables in the finished salad, otherwise they become too heavy.

Pasta with slow cooked tomatoes, Parmesan and pine kernels

1 kg tomatoes
3 tbsp chopped fresh thyme (without stalks)
Salt, sugar, pepper, olive oil
150 g pasta of your choice
30 g (3 tbsp) pine kernels
2 garlic cloves, peeled and finely chopped
2 tbsp olive oil
Basil leaves for garnishing
30 g fresh Parmesan shavings
Salt and pepper

Cut the tomatoes in half and place them in an oven tray with the cut side up. Sprinkle with a thin layer of sugar, thyme, salt and pepper. Drizzle with oil. Bake in the oven for 3-4 hours at 100°C hot air/gas ½, until the tomatoes have become wrinkled and dry on the cut side.

Boil the pasta according to the instructions on the packet, rinse in cold water and drain. Toast the pine kernels in a dry, hot pan. Mix the pasta with garlic, oil, salt and pepper.
TO SERVE Arrange the pasta on a serving dish and garnish with tomatoes, Parmesan, pine kernels and basil.

Pasta with mushrooms, hazelnuts and cranberries

A lovely autumn salad.

150 g pasta of your choice
50 g (5 tbsp) hazelnuts
500 g mushrooms, for
   example oyster mushrooms
   and field mushrooms
3 tbsp olive oil
1 generous handful fresh sage
   leaves (and a little extra)
1 garlic clove, peeled and
   finely chopped
2 tbsp white balsamic vinegar
30 g (3 tbsp) roughly chopped
   dried cranberries
Salt and pepper

Boil the pasta according to the instructions on the packet, rinse in cold water and leave to drain. Toast the roughly chopped nuts in a dry, hot pan. Cut the mushrooms into smaller pieces and toast with the sage in the oil at high temperature until the mushrooms are golden and crisp, approx. 10-15 minutes. Mix in the garlic. Mix all the ingredients and season to taste. Finally add a few fresh sage leaves.

Pasta with grilled lemon, rocket and olives

A real party salad, excellent with grilled, fried or steamed fish and our fish skewers, see page 139.

150 g pasta of your choice
1 small lemon (organic)
Olive oil
Salt and pepper
100 g large green olives,
   stone in
50 g rocket
4 tbsp olive oil
30 g fresh Parmesan shavings
   (optional)
Salt and pepper

Boil the pasta according to the instructions on the packet, rinse in cold water and leave to drain. Cut the lemon into very thin slices. Place the slices on a baking tray lined with baking paper, drizzle the olive oil over and sprinkle a little salt and pepper on top. Grill the lemon slices close to the grill element in the oven until golden, approx. 5 minutes. Chop the lemon slices when cool.

   Remove the stones from the olives and chop the flesh roughly. Mix the ingredients except for the Parmesan and a little of the lemons and season to taste. Add the last few lemon pieces.

TO SERVE Garnish with Parmesan shavings.

Pasta with slow cooked tomatoes and goat's cheese cream

1 kg tomatoes
Salt, sugar, pepper
150 g pasta of your choice
30 g (3 tbsp) pine kernels

GOAT'S CHEESE CREAM
150 g goat's cheese
   (cream cheese sort)
3 tbsp milk
4 tbsp chopped fresh basil
Salt and pepper

Cut the tomatoes in half and place them in an oven tray with the cut side up. Sprinkle with a thin layer of sugar, salt and pepper. Bake in the oven for 3-4 hours at 100°C hot air/gas ½ until the tomatoes have become wrinkled and dry on the cut side.

   Boil the pasta according to the instructions on the packet, rinse in cold water and leave to drain. Toast the pine kernels in a dry, hot pan.

GOAT'S CHEESE CREAM Mix the ingredients, add the pasta and season to taste. If necessary, the dressing may be thinned with a little extra milk, if the salad is too firm.

TO SERVE Arrange the pasta on a serving dish and garnish with tomatoes, and pine kernels.

Noodles with green beans and caramelised peanuts

150 g thin Chinese egg
   noodles
200 g fresh green beans
300 g cucumber
50 g toasted, salted peanuts
1 tbsp honey
3 hardboiled eggs, chopped

DRESSING
2 tbsp neutral tasting oil
3 tbsp lemon juice
2-3 tsp finely chopped
   red chilli (without seeds)
Salt

Boil the noodles in plenty of lightly salted water according to the instructions on the packet for approx. 2 minutes, rinse in cold water and leave to drain. Trim the beans and steam in a saucepan under a lid in a little lightly salted water until almost tender, approx. 3 minutes. Rinse immediately in cold water. Cut the beans lengthways with a sharp vegetable knife. Cut the cucumber lengthways, remove the seeds with a teaspoon and cut into slices of approx. ½ cm. Heat the nuts in a dry, hot pan, add the honey and stir until the honey has melted. Leave the nuts on a plate to cool.

Mix the ingredients for the dressing with the noodles and the beans. Season the salad to taste.

TO SERVE Mix in the sliced cucumber and garnish with peanuts and chopped hardboiled eggs.

Noodles with spinach and toasted cashew nuts

This salad is excellent with lean pork and poultry. The cashew nuts are available toasted and salted from most supermarkets

150 g thin Chinese egg
   noodles
400 g fresh spinach,
   preferably baby spinach
100 g toasted, salted cashew
   nuts (or peanuts)

DRESSING
3 tbsp neutral tasting oil
4 tbsp freshly squeezed
   lime juice
10 finely chopped lime leaves
1 garlic clove, peeled and
   finely chopped
2 tbsp finely grated fresh
   ginger
Salt and pepper

Boil the noodles in plenty of lightly salted water according to the instructions on the packet, approx. 2 minutes, rinse in cold water and leave to drain. Rinse the spinach in several lots of clean water, leave to drain. Ordinary spinach should be roughly chopped. Baby spinach should be left as it is. Mix the ingredients for the dressing directly with the noodles.
TO SERVE Add spinach and roughly ground nuts and season to taste.

Buckwheat noodles with crisp vegetables and peanut cream

Japanese buckwheat noodles are available from Asian grocers or health food shops.

100 g buckwheat noodles
1 bunch (approx 125 g)
   radishes
150 g carrot
200 g yellow pepper
100 g sugar snaps
1 small bunch chives

PEANUT CREAM
3 tbsp crunchy peanut butter
1 garlic clove, peeled and
   crushed
2 tbsp freshly squeezed
   lime juice (or lemon juice)
2 tbsp soy sauce
2 tsp maple syrup
   (or clear honey)
½ tsp ground cumin
Approx. 1 tsp water
Cayenne pepper

Place the noodles in a pot of unsalted, boiling water. Stir the noodles to begin with to avoid them sticking together. Boil for approx. 5 minutes, to al dente. Pour the noodles into a sieve, rinse in cold water and leave to drain. Remove the top of the radishes and slice thinly. Peel and cut the carrots into thin strips. Remove the seeds from the pepper and cut the flesh into thin strips. Cut the peas finely diagonally across.

Whisk all the ingredients for the peanut cream and season to taste, it should be sweet-sour-quite strong.

Mix buckwheat noodles and vegetables. You could also, as shown in the photo the way they serve the noodles in Japan, roll the noodles into bird nests with a fork and garnish with the remaining ingredients. Drizzle the cream over and garnish with chopped chives.

BUCKWHEAT NOODLES WITH CRISP VEGE-
TABLES AND PEANUT CREAM

Rice noodles and prawns in sweet and sour sauce

100 g rice noodles
200 g peeled frozen prawns
1 kg (1 small) ripe
    fresh pineapple
1 bunch of spring onions
1 pot roughly chopped fresh
    coriander (optional)

SWEET AND SOUR SAUCE
2 tbsp tomato ketchup
4 tsp white wine vinegar
1 tbsp muscovado sugar
    (or soft brown sugar)
1 garlic clove, peeled and
    finely chopped
1 tbsp finely grated fresh
    ginger
½ tsp ground anise seed
2 tbsp neutral tasting oil
Salt and pepper

Defrost the prawns, preferably overnight in the fridge so they lose less juice. Boil the noodles in plenty of lightly salted water according to the instructions on the packet, approx. 2 minutes, rinse in cold water and leave to drain. Cut the top off and peel the pineapple, cut away the hard centre and cut the flesh into small cubes. Remove the outer discoloured leaves from the spring onions and one third of the top. Cut into slices diagonally of approx. ½ cm and rinse thoroughly. Place the spring onions in a sieve, pour over boiling water and leave for a couple of minutes, then drain.

SWEET AND SOUR SAUCE Whisk the ingredients thoroughly except for the oil until the sugar has dissolved. Finally mix in the oil. Mix all the ingredients with the dressing and season to taste.

Bulgur with baked courgettes, aubergines and toasted walnuts

1 kg courgettes and
    aubergines (total weight)
4 tbsp olive oil
2 tsp dried mint
1 tsp ground allspice
Salt and pepper
1 garlic clove, peeled and
    finely chopped
200 g bulgur
300 ml boiling water
50 g walnuts
3 tbsp freshly squeezed
    lemon juice
10 tbsp finely chopped parsley

Cut the vegetables into cubes of 1 x 1 cm. Place in an oven tray lined with baking paper and mix with oil and spices. Bake in the oven for approx. ½ hour at 175°C hot air/gas 6 until crisp and tender. Turn them over several times during cooking. Mix in the garlic when the vegetables have been cooked. Pour boiling water over the bulgur and leave for ½ hour under a lid, leave to cool. Rinse with cold water and drain. Toast the walnuts in a dry, hot pan and chop them roughly.

TO SERVE Mix all the ingredients and season to taste.

Bulgur with herbs and caramelised pistachio nuts

250 g bulgur
1 large pinch of saffron
50 g red salad onion
1 garlic clove, peeled and
    finely chopped
5 tbsp finely chopped parsley
10 tbsp chopped fresh
    coriander, (or use parsley
    and add a little extra)
100 g salted pistachio nuts
    in their shell
1 tbsp honey
Salt and pepper
4 tbsp olive oil
2 tbsp freshly squeezed
    lemon juice

Pour boiling water over the bulgur and saffron and leave for ½ hour under a lid, leave to cool. Rinse with cold water and leave to drain in a fine mesh sieve. Chop the onion finely. Shell and chop the nuts roughly and heat them thoroughly in a hot pan together with the honey. Leave to cool on a plate.
TO SERVE Mix all the ingredients and season the salad to taste.

Noodles with oyster mushrooms and sesame omelette

You can also make the salad without the noodles, simply add 300 g extra vegetables, for example leeks, or green peppers cut into strips.

150 g Chinese egg noodles
3 eggs
2 tbsp milk
2 tsp sesame seeds
Salt and pepper
1 + 1 tbsp neutral tasting oil
300 g leeks
500 g oyster mushrooms
    (or other type of mushroom)
2 garlic cloves, peeled and
    finely chopped
2 tsp dark Chinese sesame oil
2 tbsp white balsamic vinegar
    (or rice wine vinegar)

Boil the noodles in plenty of lightly salted water according to the instructions on the packet, approx. 2 minutes, rinse in cold water and leave to drain. Whisk eggs, milk, sesame seeds, salt and pepper. Fry the egg mixture in 1 tbsp oil at medium heat in a large pan without lid for approx. 5 minutes each side, until the omelette is golden.

Cut the leeks including the tops into slices of approx. 10 cm, cut these into rough strips lengthways and rinse thoroughly in several lots of cold water. Cut the mushrooms into smaller bits and toast in 1 tbsp oil at high temperature until golden, approx. 10-15 minutes. Add the garlic and leeks and fry for a further 5 minutes.

Mix all the ingredients except for the omelette. Roll up the omelette and cut it into narrow strips. Mix half the strips carefully with the other ingredients and use the rest to garnish.

Spelt salad with fried plums, mushrooms and rosemary

Goes well with fried duck breast, roast pork, meatballs and salmon. Try it also with goat's cheese or feta cheese sprinkled over the dish.

125 g whole spelt
Good quality vegetable stock
 or water
250 g Portobello mushrooms
 (or other mushrooms)
250 g red onion
3 sprigs of fresh rosemary,
 stripped
4 tsp olive oil
400 g plums
2 tbsp balsamic vinegar
Salt and pepper

Boil the spelt in the vegetable stock or water according to the instructions on the packet. Pour the spelt into a sieve and leave to drain. Do not wash the mushrooms but wipe them with kitchen towel or brush them with a pastry brush. Cut into smaller pieces. Peel the onion and cut it into thin wedges. Line a baking tray with baking paper, place the onions and mushrooms on the tray, mix with rosemary, oil, salt and pepper and bake in the oven at 175°C hot air/gas 6 for approx. 20 minutes, until browned and tender. Turn the vegetables once during cooking.

Cut the plums in half, remove the stones and cut the plums into smaller wedges. Turn the oven up to 200°C hot air/gas 7, mix the plums with the mushrooms and onion and bake for a further approx. 10 minutes. Mix the mushrooms, onion and plums with the boiled spelt, vinegar, salt and pepper and season to taste.

Quinoa-tabbouleh with citrus fruit, pine kernels and herbs

Excellent with lamb, poultry and fish. Read about the 'gold grain' quinoa on page 11.

150 g whole quinoa
350 ml water
1 (approx 250 g) (red)
   grapefruit
2 (approx 350 g) oranges
100 g dried apricots
   (or figs)
30 g pine kernels
2 handfuls herbs
   for example mint, coriander,
   broad leaved parsley
Salt

DRESSING

1 tbsp lemon juice
1 tbsp good olive oil
1 garlic clove, peeled and
   crushed
1 pinch cayenne pepper,
   or to taste
Salt

Rinse the quinoa in cold water in a sieve. Boil the quinoa in the water in a saucepan under a lid at low temperature for 10 minutes, remove from the heat, add salt, stir and leave in the saucepan with a lid for 10 minutes, or longer, to ensure all the water has been absorbed and the grain is soft and loose. Peel and remove the white pith from the grapefruit, cut into quarters, remove the white membranes in the middle and cut the flesh into smaller pieces. Remove the peel and membranes from the orange and cut it into smaller pieces, remove also the white membranes in the middle. Cut the apricots into thin slices.

Toast the pine kernels until golden in a dry, hot pan. Pinch the leaves off the herbs, rinse and dry. Mix the quinoa with the ingredients for the dressing and half the citrus fruits and apricots. Season to taste and arrange on a serving dish.

TO SERVE Chop the herbs roughly. Garnish with the rest of the citrus fruits, herbs, pine kernels and apricots.

White and green beans with anchovy mayonnaise

Anchovies in oil have a strong flavour and are used as a spice in cooking. Many people have the idea that they do not like anchovies but try this salad, it is fabulous. The anchovies are available from well stocked supermarkets and Italian speciality shops. Good mayonnaise is available from health food shops and the best supermarkets.

200 g dried white beans
250 g fresh green beans
1 large handful chopped broad leaved parsley

ANCHOVY MAYONNAISE

4 tbsp good quality mayonnaise
1 garlic clove, peeled and crushed
1 tbsp white wine vinegar
30 g drained (approx. 8) anchovy fillets
A little salt and a lot of pepper

Soak the beans overnight in plenty of cold water. Drain and boil in fresh water with a little salt for approx. 1 hour until tender and leave to cool.

ANCHOVY MAYONNAISE Chop the anchovy fillets very finely and mix in the mayonnaise. Mix in the white beans and set aside for at least ½ hour. Trim the green beans and steam them under a lid in a little salted water until almost tender, approx. 3 minutes. Rinse immediately in cold water.

TO SERVE Mix in the green beans and parsley and season to taste.

VARIATION 1 Replace green beans with 250 g cherry tomatoes cut in half, add 2 tsp only of white wine vinegar.

VARIATION 2 Replace with basil-mayonnaise: Replace anchovies and parsley with a large handful of chopped fresh basil and the zest of ½ lemon. Use 2 cloves of garlic instead of 1.

Bean salads

There are fresh beans and dried beans. The dried beans come from many different types of legumes, which are dried and podded in their country of origin. The dried beans and lentils are quite heavy, very filling and are a meal in themselves served with bread or a light green salad. Some people find them a bit of a bother because they have to be soaked for a long time in cold water. You can use butter beans, mung beans and lentils instead which do not need soaking before cooking. Always use at least 50% boiled beans and 50% vegetables in a dish.

SONJA'S FAVOURITE SALAD

Sonja's favourite salad

This is a substantial salad which can easily be a meal in itself for lunch or as the side dish with fish or meat served with bread. If the apple is very sweet add a little more balsamic vinegar.

50 g walnuts
2 tsp honey
250 g red or orange peppers
2 tbsp olive oil
1 garlic clove, peeled and
   finely chopped
1 tbsp balsamic vinegar
300 g fresh green beans
150 g slightly sour apple
1 bunch of watercress
Salt and pepper

Toast the nuts with a little salt in a dry, hot pan. Add honey and mix it well. Leave the nuts to cool on a plate. Cut the peppers into cubes of 1 x 1 cm, and fry at medium heat with salt and lots of pepper for approx. 5-6 minutes, until browned and soft. Add garlic, mix it well, add vinegar, mix it in and remove the pan from the heat. Trim the beans and steam them under a lid in a little salted water until almost tender, approx. 3 minutes. Rinse immediately in cold water. Remove the core and cut the apple into cubes of 1 x 1 cm. Mix apples, peppers and beans carefully together and season the salad to taste.

TO SERVE Chop the watercress and sprinkle it over the dish, toss the salad and arrange it on a serving dish. Break the walnuts into smaller bits and use for garnishing.

Green beans with a crunchy mint hazelnut pesto

If you prefer you can replace the mint with parsley and add 50 g good quality crumbled feta cheese.

500 g fresh green beans
50 g hazelnuts
2 tbsp olive oil
3 tbsp finely chopped
   fresh mint
1 garlic clove, peeled and
   finely chopped
2 tsp freshly squeezed
   lemon juice
1 generous pinch of cayenne
   pepper
Salt

Trim the beans and steam under a lid in a little salted water until almost tender, approx. 3 minutes. Rinse immediately in cold water. Toast the hazelnuts in a dry, hot pan and chop them roughly.

Mix in all the ingredients and season to taste.

Beans & rice salad

Mung beans are a positive surprise, both in terms of flavour and because they need very little cooking time. The beans do not have to be soaked. However, they easily become mushy, so add salt or a good vegetable stock. You can use either beans or rice, or both. Beans and rice together provide nutritionally a complete meal. The salad is also delicious on its own, when the beans and rice are served either hot or lukewarm. You can replace carrots, spinach and avocado with all kinds of vegetables – empty your fridge.

75 g mung beans
75 g brown basmati rice
Salt or possibly
   vegetable stock for boiling
2 (150 g) carrots
1 ripe avocado
50 g fresh spinach
(optional)

MARINADE

3 tbsp apple cider vinegar
1 tbsp maple syrup
2 tbsp soy sauce
1 garlic clove, peeled and
   crushed
Cayenne pepper to taste

TOPPING

½ tsp cumin seeds
1 tbsp (10 g) sesame seeds
2 tbsp (15 g) pumpkin seeds
Fresh coriander (optional)

Rinse the beans and the rice in a sieve. Boil together in plenty of water with salt or stock cubes/powder for 15-20 minutes until tender. Keep an eye on the beans for the last 5 minutes as they suddenly become mushy. Remove the saucepan from the heat and leave for 5-10 minutes, then drain off the water. Mix the marinade, make it quite strong and mix it with rice and beans, while they are still warm. Peel and cut the carrots into small cubes and add to the salad. Cut the avocado into small cubes and mix with the salad, season to taste.

Crush the cumin seeds lightly with a mortar and pestle or with a sharp knife. Toast the cumin seeds, sesame seeds and the pumpkin seeds in a dry, hot pan stirring all the time. Rinse the spinach in several lots of water, dry it thoroughly in a salad spinner.
TO SERVE Mix the spinach with the salad and sprinkle the topping over.

Energy bomb salad

– with two kinds of beans and two kinds of seaweed. Read about seaweed and edamame beans on page 12. If necessary, you can use one kind of seaweed only. The green beans could be replaced with an extra bunch of radishes.

1 handful (10 g) wakame
  seaweed
1 handful (10 g) arame
  seaweed
1 bag (454 g) edamame beans
  in their pod
150 g green beans
1 bunch (125 g) radishes

DRESSING
½ - 1 tsp wasabi from a tube
2 tsp clear honey
Finely grated zest of
  ½ organic lemon
4 tsp lemon juice
2 tbsp soy sauce

Place the seaweed in a bowl and pour over boiling water, leave for approx. 10 minutes, then leave to drain in a sieve. Mix the dressing and pour it over the seaweed. Leave to marinate for as long as possible. Pour the frozen edamame beans into boiling water and boil for 3-4 minutes, after the water has returned to boiling point, until the beans are crisp inside. Taste the beans (the beans, not the pod); they should be al dente. Pod the green beans. Trim the green beans and boil them in lightly salted water for approx. 3-5 minutes until they are al dente. Put them in a sieve and rinse in cold water. Remove the top of the radishes and slice them thinly.

TO SERVE Mix the vegetables and the marinated seaweed, season the salad to taste.

The Hit List

These are our own favourites.
Begin here if you don't know
what to serve.

Arabic slaw
PAGE 30

Baked aubergines with
yoghurt and honey
PAGE 97

Sonja's favourite salad
PAGE 67

Beans & rice salad
PAGE 68

Indian inspired
potato salad
PAGE 50

Salads with strawberries
and elderflowers
PAGE 84

Peperonata cream
PAGE 122

Potato salad with
mushrooms, spinach
and miso dressing
PAGE 48

Baked Hamburg
parsley with
clementines and linseed
PAGE 38

Oranges with olives
and cream
PAGE 110

Chinese inspired duck
breast salad
PAGE 106

Green salads

Green salads make excellent first courses, since, apart from being very delicate, they can also be prepared in advance and be ready on the table; (not too early, however, or they will go limp). The dressing for green salads should be mixed with the salad only just before serving otherwise it goes limp.

LOLLA BIONADA
MILD, SWEET, LIGHTLY
SPICY FLAVOUR

**GREEN CURLY
(OR GREEN OAK LEAF)**
MILD NUTTY FLAVOUR

**RED MANGOLD
(OR RED BEET LEAF)**
MILD TASTE OF BEETROOT

LITTLE GEM LETTUCE
SWEET, MILD
AND CRISP

RADICCHIO
STRONG, BITTER
SWEET TASTE, GOOD IN
SALAD MIXES

ICEBERG
MILD AND CRISP

BABY SPINACH
FULL OF
VITAMINS

CORN SALAD
MILD, SPICY
NUTTY FLAVOUR

**RED CURLY
(OR RED OAK LEAF)**
MILD NUTTY FLAVOUR

RED MIZUNA
MILD, LIGHTLY
SPICY
FLAVOUR

76 GREEN SALADS

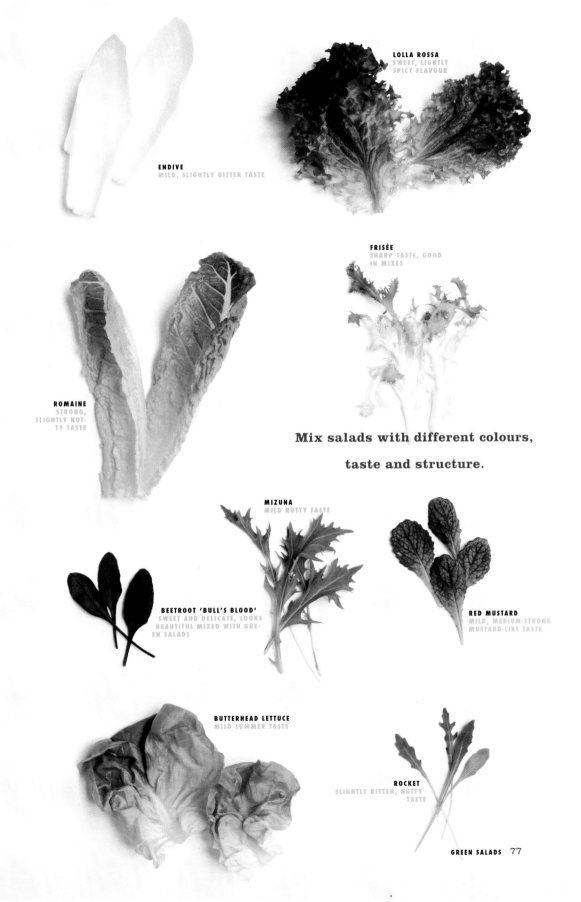

LOLLA ROSSA
SWEET, LIGHTLY
SPICY FLAVOUR

ENDIVE
MILD, SLIGHTLY BITTER TASTE

FRISÉE
SHARP TASTE, GOOD
IN MIXES

ROMAINE
STRONG,
SLIGHTLY NUT-
TY TASTE

Mix salads with different colours,

taste and structure.

MIZUNA
MILD NUTTY TASTE

BEETROOT 'BULL'S BLOOD'
SWEET AND DELICATE, LOOKS
BEAUTIFUL MIXED WITH GRE-
EN SALADS

RED MUSTARD
MILD, MEDIUM-STRONG
MUSTARD-LIKE TASTE

BUTTERHEAD LETTUCE
MILD SUMMER TASTE

ROCKET
SLIGHTLY BITTER, NUTTY
TASTE

Green salad with Hamburg parsley chips and blueberries

Goes well with loin of beef or steaks. Make a large portion of Hamburg parsley chips and have them as snacks.

100 g Hamburg parsley
   or parsnip
1 tbsp olive oil
200 g baby leaves of your
   own choice
125 g blueberries or
   blackberries
Salt and pepper

DRESSING
2 tbsp concentrated blueberry
   or blackcurrant juice
4 tsp balsamic vinegar
Salt and pepper

Peel the parsnips and cut them into thin slices using a potato peeler. Mix with oil, salt and pepper in a bowl. Place in a thin layer on a baking tray lined with baking paper and bake in the oven at 200°C hot air/gas 7 for 3-5 minutes until golden and crisp. Keep an eye on them as they easily burn. Leave to cool. Rinse and dry the salad, rinse the berries. Mix the dressing and season to taste, add the berries.
TO SERVE Arrange the salad on a serving dish, pour the berry dressing over and top with the parsnip chips.

Granny's dressing with variations

Here are three variations on the traditional summer salad with lemon-cream dressing. We break with one of our sacred principles by mixing butterhead lettuce, which is a summer vegetable, with oranges which are winter fruits. But please note there are no rules without exceptions in the service of flavour.

Granny's dressing with orange

3-400 g butterhead lettuce
3 oranges

DRESSING
5 tbsp whipping cream
1 tbsp freshly squeezed
   orange juice
1 tsp freshly squeezed
   lemon juice
1½ tsp sugar
Salt and pepper

Rinse the lettuce and tear it into mouth-size pieces. Peel the orange and cut it into segments or smaller pieces. Mix the dressing thoroughly. **TO SERVE** Mix salad, dressing and half the orange pieces in a bowl. Garnish with the rest of the oranges.

Granny's dressing with rocket

200 g rocket
3 oranges
30 g (3 tbsp) toasted pine
   kernels

DRESSING
4 tbsp whipping cream
1 tbsp olive oil
1 tbsp freshly squeezed
   orange juice
1 tsp freshly squeezed
   lemon juice
1½ tsp sugar
Salt and pepper

Rinse the salad. Peel the orange and cut it into segments or smaller pieces. Toast the pine kernels in a dry, hot pan until golden. Mix the dressing thoroughly. **TO SERVE** Mix the salad, dressing and half the orange in a bowl. Garnish with the rest of the orange and pine kernels.

Granny's dressing with strawberries

3-400 g butterhead lettuce
250 g strawberries

DRESSING
5 tbsp whipping cream
4 tsp freshly squeezed
   lemon juice
1½ tsp sugar
Salt and pepper

Rinse the lettuce and tear it into mouth-size pieces. Hull the strawberries and cut them into halves. Mix the dressing thoroughly. **TO SERVE** Mix the salad, dressing and half the strawberries in a bowl. Garnish with the rest of the strawberries.

CUTTING CITRUS FILLETS

Arabic inspired Caesar salad

The traditional Caesar salad is American and consists of Romaine lettuce, garlic croutons, Parmesan cheese, anchovy fillets and a thin mayonnaise dressing.

The salad is typically served as a first course or as a lunch dish. Here are two variations on the theme.

3-400 g Romaine lettuce
80 g feta cheese
1 tbsp freshly squeezed
    lemon juice
Pepper

OREGANO CROUTONS

100 g dried white bread with
    crust (preferably
    Italian bread)
3 tbsp olive oil
1 tbsp dried oregano
½ tsp ground cumin
2 garlic cloves, peeled and
    finely chopped
Salt and pepper

Rinse the lettuce and tear it into mouth-size pieces. Cut the bread into cubes of approx. ½ x ½ cm. Mix oil and spices (except for the garlic) with the bread cubes. Fry in a pan over a medium heat, until golden, approx. 5 minutes. Add garlic, and fry for a bit more, take care it doesn't burn. Leave the croutons to cool.
TO SERVE Arrange the salad in a bowl, add the lemon juice, crumble the cheese over and garnish with the croutons.

Mexican inspired Caesar salad

3-400 g Romaine lettuce
Approx. 50 g roughly chopped
    Jalapeño chillies
    (available in slices in jars)
1 tbsp freshly squeezed
    lemon juice

CORIANDER CROUTONS

100 g dried white bread
1 tsp ground coriander
½ tsp ground anise seed
1 pinch ground cinnamon
Salt
2 garlic cloves, peeled and
    finely chopped
50 g grated red Cheddar
    cheese

Rinse the lettuce and tear it into mouth-size pieces. Cut the bread into cubes of approx. ½ x ½ cm. Mix with the spices and fry in a pan at medium temperature, until golden, approx. 5 minutes. Add garlic, and fry for a bit more, take care it doesn't burn. Arrange the croutons on a plate and grate the cheese over. Leave to cool
TO SERVE Mix the chilli and lemon juice with the salad and arrange the croutons on top.

Iceberg salad with cherries, toasted almonds and lemon zest

It is important that the stalk remains on the cherries so people are aware that they still have the stones in. The salad should be made during the summer, June-August when salads and cherries are in high season.

3-400 g iceberg lettuce
200 g fresh cherries with
    stones and stalk
50 g almonds
The zest of 1 organic lemon

DRESSING

5 tbsp whipping cream
4 tsp freshly squeezed
    lemon juice or (cherry)
    vinegar
1½ tsp sugar
Salt and pepper

Rinse the lettuce and tear it into mouth-size pieces. Toast the almonds in a dry, hot pan until golden. Chop the almonds roughly. Grate the lemons with a citrus zester and mix the dressing.
TO SERVE Mix the salad with the dressing and garnish with the other ingredients.

Salad with goat's cheese, honey and walnuts

If you are not fond of goat's cheese, brie may be used instead.

200 g mixed green leaves of your choice
50 g walnuts
1½ tbsp balsamic vinegar
1 tbsp olive oil
100 g firm white goat's cheese (or mild brie)
2 tsp clear honey
Salt and pepper

Rinse the lettuce and tear it into mouth-size pieces. Toast the nuts in a dry, hot pan until golden. Cut into smaller pieces, if necessary.

TO SERVE Mix the salad with balsamic vinegar, oil, salt and pepper and arrange on a serving dish. Slice the cheese thinly and arrange over the salad. Finally spoon the nuts and honey over the salad.

Salad with spicy nuts

The nuts can be varied with different spices ad infinitum. You will need 2-3 tsp ground spice to each 100 g nuts. Try also nutmeg, cinnamon, ginger and cloves.

200 g mixed green leaves of
   your choice
100 g nuts of your choice,
   for example walnuts,
   hazelnuts, almonds,
   pine kernels, cashew nuts,
   pistachio nuts
1½ tsp ground cumin
1½ tsp ground coriander
½ tsp turmeric
1 generous pinch chilli
   powder or cayenne pepper
2 tbsp honey
Salt

DRESSING
1 tbsp neutral tasting oil
1 tbsp freshly squeezed
   lemon juice
1 garlic clove, peeled and
   finely chopped
Salt

Rinse the lettuce and tear it into mouth-size pieces. Toast the nuts in a dry, hot pan, remove the pan from the heat and add spices and salt. Put the pan on the heat again, add honey and warm it through. Leave the nuts to cool on a plate. Mix the dressing. Break the nuts with your fingers and break/chop the biggest into smaller pieces.

TO SERVE Mix the dressing with the salad and arrange the nuts on top.

Salads with strawberries and elderflowers

This is a real summer salad. Make it when strawberries
are in peak season from June-August. It is also then that
summer lettuce is most crisp and has the best flavour.
The salad is very beautiful and is particularly suitable for
romantic summer parties. The dressing is fantastic and tastes
wonderful on its own in green salads.

3-400 g Iceberg lettuce and/
  or 200 g baby leaves
250 g strawberries
30 g (3 tbsp) pine kernels
Salt
1 tbsp concentrated
  elderflower juice
1 handful red and pink rose
  leaves pesticide-free from
  the garden (optional)

ELDERFLOWER DRESSING
2 tbsp lemon-olive oil
  (or 2 tbsp olive oil and 2 tsp
  finely grated lemon zest)
1 tbsp freshly squeezed
  lemon juice
1 tbsp concentrated
  elderflower juice

Rinse the lettuce and tear it
into mouth-size pieces. Toast
the pine kernels in a dry,
hot pan until golden. Add salt
and elderflower juice and leave
the juice to steam off. Leave to
cool on a plate. Cut the
strawberries into quarters.
If necessary leave 'the stalk'
on the strawberries. Mix the
dressing thoroughly.

TO SERVE Mix the dressing with
the salad and arrange it on a
serving dish. Garnish with
strawberries, pine kernels and
rose leaves, if available.

Asparagus salads

Much of the imported asparagus can be a bit woody. Use local varieties when in season, if you can get hold of them. You can use white asparagus in the salads, but we believe the green ones suit these recipes best.

ASPARAGUS WITH EGG, SPINACH AND TAPENADE

Asparagus with egg, spinach and tapenade

500 g (1 bunch) green
   asparagus
2 eggs
50 g (1 handful) baby spinach
   or other green leaves
A little fresh chervil (optional)

TAPENADE

100 g black olives, stones out
1 tbsp capers
2 tbsp olive oil
1 tbsp lemon juice
1 garlic clove
Pepper

Remove the bottom woody
part from the asparagus.
Steam in a little salted water
under a tight fitting lid, for
3-5 minutes until tender but
still al dente. Rinse with cold
water and leave to drain.
Boil the eggs until hardboiled,
8-9 minutes. Cut the eggs into
quarters. Wash the spinach
thoroughly in several lots of
clean water.

Blend all the ingredients for
the tapenade in a food
processor or chop it all finely.

TO SERVE Arrange the spinach
on a serving dish, spoon over
a third of the tapenade,
then the asparagus and the
rest of the tapenade. Garnish
with hardboiled egg and a
little chervil.

Baked asparagus with Parma ham and Parmesan

500 g (1 bunch) green
   asparagus
70 g (1 packet) sliced
   Parma ham
Olive oil
1 head of radicchio
30 g fresh Parmesan shavings

DRESSING

2 tbsp lemon-olive oil
   (or 2 tbsp olive oil and
    2 tsp finely grated zest of
    an organic lemon)
2 tsp lemon juice
Salt and pepper

Remove the bottom woody
part from the asparagus.
Cut the Parma ham into
3 pieces diagonally. Wrap the
Parma ham round the
asparagus. If there is not
enough for all the asparagus
just bake the rest without the
ham. Place on a baking tray
lined with baking paper and
drizzle with olive oil. Bake at
175°C hot air/gas 6 for
approx. 10 minutes until they
are golden.

Tear the radicchio into
mouth-size pieces and rinse
thoroughly. Mix the dressing,
taking care with the salt as
the ham is salty.

TO SERVE Arrange the salad on a
serving dish with the
asparagus first, then pour the
dressing over and finally the
Parmesan shavings using a
potato peeler.

Tomato salads

For the best flavour use cherry tomatoes and tomatoes on the vine which are ripened on the plant instead of ripening after picking. Tomato salads should be eaten fresh, immediately after preparation.

Tomatoes with 3 kinds of cheese

750 g tomatoes on the vine
Balsamic vinegar
Salt
60 g fresh mozzarella
   (if possible made from
   buffalo milk)
20 g fresh Parmesan shavings
30 g Gorgonzola
   (or other Italian cheeses of
   your choice)
Pepper
Olive oil

Slice the tomatoes and arrange them in a serving dish. Drizzle a little balsamic vinegar over (not too much). Sprinkle with salt. Slice the cheeses thinly, cut the Parmesan with a potato peeler and arrange the cheeses on top of the tomatoes. Drizzle with olive oil and grate black pepper on top.

Italian inspired tomato and bread salad

It is very important that both bread and oil are of the highest quality.

100 g dried Italian durum wheat bread
400 g tomatoes on the vine
2 garlic cloves, peeled and finely chopped
3 tbsp olive oil
2 tbsp white wine vinegar
1 small handful chopped fresh parsley
1 small handful (½ pot) chopped fresh basil
Salt and pepper

Slice the bread and break it into small pieces. Cut the tomatoes into cubes of approx. 1 x 1 cm. Mix with the other ingredients and season to taste.

Tomato salad à la Mexico

Remember to start this salad the day before you want to eat it, as the dried beans need soaking.

100 g dried kidney beans (or 200 g tinned, warmed)
Salt
2-3 tsp chopped jalapeño chillies (available in slices in jars)
1 tbsp neutral tasting oil
1 garlic clove, peeled and finely chopped
400 g cherry tomatoes

SWEETCORN CREAM
100 g Greek yoghurt 10% fat
100 g sweetcorn (or loose corn kernels from 1 boiled corn on the cob)
2 tbsp chopped fresh coriander
Salt and pepper

Soak the beans overnight, drain off the water and boil them in fresh lightly salted water until soft and tender but not over-cooked approx. ½-1 hour. Marinade in oil, garlic and chilli (while the beans are still warm) and season to taste. Cut the tomatoes into halves. Mix the sweetcorn cream and season to taste.
TO SERVE: Mix tomatoes and beans. Arrange in a serving dish. Spoon the cream over the mixture.

Tomatoes with horseradish cream

Goes well with poultry, beef or any other dish with which you would traditionally serve horseradish sauce.

1 kg tomatoes on the vine
1 tbsp freshly grated horseradish
Chopped parsley to garnish

HORSERADISH CREAM
200 g Greek yoghurt 10% fat
2 tbsp whole, finely grated horseradish
1 tsp sugar
1 tsp white balsamic vinegar (or white wine vinegar)
Salt and pepper

Mix the horseradish cream and set aside for ½ hour. Slice the tomatoes and arrange them in a serving dish. Spoon the cream over the tomatoes. Sprinkle with grated horseradish and parsley.

Cherry tomatoes and Jerusalem artichokes in peanut cream

Jerusalem artichoke on its own in a salad is far too heavy – impossible to chew your way through and digest. It is best in a combination with less fibrous vegetables such as tomatoes.

150 g leeks
500 g Jerusalem artichokes
250 g cherry tomatoes

PEANUT CREAM
5 tbsp peanut butter
1 garlic clove, peeled and
   finely chopped
200 ml natural yoghurt
1 generous pinch of
   cayenne pepper
Salt

Cut the leeks into julienne strips, rinse them thoroughly in several lots of clean water, pour boiling water over and set aside for approx.1 minute. Drain off the water. Mix the cream, remove the dark tips from the Jerusalem artichokes, peel them with a potato peeler and slice them as thinly as possible. Mix with the cream immediately or they will discolour. Arrange on a serving dish, add the cherry tomatoes and finally the leek strips.

VARIATION Some or all the Jerusalem artichokes may be replaced with sliced boiled potatoes or potatoes cut into smaller pieces.

Tomatoes with fried peppers and mozzarella

400 g red and yellow peppers
2 tbsp olive oil
2 garlic cloves, peeled and
   finely chopped
2 tbsp balsamic vinegar
600 g tomatoes on the vine
100 g fresh mozzarella
   (from buffalo milk,
   if available)
Fresh basil for garnishing
Salt and pepper

Cut each pepper into 6-8 wedges. Remove the seeds. Fry over a medium heat in the oil with salt and pepper in a pan for approx. 15 minutes, until browned and tender. Add garlic at the last minute and finish by drizzling balsamic vinegar over the vegetables. Slice the tomatoes, sprinkle with a little more salt and pepper, if necessary, cut the cheese into thin slices and then cut in half.
TO SERVE Arrange in a serving dish. Place tomatoes, peppers and mozzarella in layers and garnish with basil leaves.

TOMATOES WITH FRIED PEPPERS AND MOZZARELLA

Salads with avocado, peppers, aubergine or pumpkin

Baked pumpkin with tarragon

Goes well with poultry and beef.

1 (800 g) Japanese kabocha
  pumpkin
2 tbsp olive oil
1 large handful roughly
  chopped tarragon
Salt

SALSA
250 g cherry tomatoes
1 yellow pepper
½-1 green chilli
1 garlic clove, peeled and
  crushed
2 tbsp white wine vinegar
  (or white balsamic vinegar)
Salt

Wash the pumpkin, cut in half and remove the seeds, leave the peel on, it is delicious, and cut the pumpkin into small wedges. For this you will need a sharp knife. Place the wedges in a bowl and mix them thoroughly with oil, tarragon and salt. Place in one layer on a baking tray lined with baking paper and bake in a hot air oven at 250°C hot air/gas 9 for 10-12 minutes until they are just about tender.

SALSA Cut the tomatoes into quarters, cut away seeds and membranes from the peppers and cut the peppers into small cubes. Cut the chilli into tiny cubes, discarding the seeds and the membranes. For the salsa mix tomatoes, pepper, chilli, garlic, vinegar and salt and season to taste – it should be reasonably acidic.

TO SERVE Arrange the pumpkin slices on a serving dish, and spoon the salsa on top.

Baked peppers with rocket-vinaigrette

1.3 kg red and yellow peppers
1½ tbsp olive oil
Salt and pepper

VINAIGRETTE
1 small bunch rocket,
    approx. 35 g
½ tbsp capers
2 cloves of garlic
3 tbsp olive oil
1 tbsp balsamic vinegar
Salt and pepper

Cut the peppers into halves, remove the seeds and place them in a baking tray lined with baking paper, brush with oil and sprinkle with salt and pepper. Bake in the oven at 200°C hot air/gas 7 for approx. 45 minutes until golden and tender. Turn them over half way through the cooking time.
VINAIGRETTE Chop capers, garlic and rocket finely. Mix with the other ingredients and season to taste.
TO SERVE Arrange the peppers on a serving dish, and spoon the vinaigrette over.

VARIATION
Baked peppers with radicchio

Arrange leaves of radicchio at the bottom of the dish, drizzle half of the vinaigrette over, then the peppers and finally the rest of the vinaigrette.

Fried aubergines and radishes with miso dressing

This is a Japanese inspired salad. The Japanese use aubergines also with miso and normally Chinese radish, here replaced with beautiful local radishes. Goes well with lean fish and meat. Read about the healthy and flavoursome miso on page 11.

2 (approx 700 g) aubergines
Neutral tasting oil for
    brushing on the vegetables
1 bunch (approx 125 g)
    radishes
1 small bunch chives
Salt

MISO DRESSING
4 tbsp miso, light or dark
Zest of 1 organic lime
2 tbsp freshly squeezed
    lime juice
1 garlic clove, peeled and
    crushed
1½ tbsp maple syrup
    (or honey)
A little water, if necessary

Slice the aubergines into 1 cm thick slices and place on a baking tray lined with baking paper. Brush with oil, sprinkle with salt and bake the aubergine slices in the oven at 200°C hot air/gas 7 for approx. 25 minutes, until golden and tender. You do not need to turn them over.

Remove the top of the radishes and cut them into slices. Chop the chives into smaller pieces. Mix the dressing and season to taste. Add a little water if you think the dressing is too thick. Place the fried aubergines on a large serving dish and sprinkle the radishes over.
TO SERVE Drizzle the miso dressing over and garnish with chives.

We bake the peppers in the oven or fry them in a pan, but we do not remove the skin as is the norm in many classic Italian recipes. They taste delicious with the skin left on.

FRIED AUBERGINES AND RADISHES
WITH MISO DRESSING

BAKED AUBERGINES
WITH YOGHURT AND HONEY

Baked aubergines with yoghurt and honey

The salad is prettier without the parsley but it tastes better with.

1 kg aubergines
6 tbsp olive oil
200 ml natural yoghurt
2 garlic cloves, peeled and
   finely chopped
2 tsp honey
1 large handful chopped
   broad leaved parsley
Salt and pepper

Cut the aubergines diagonally into slices of approx. 1 cm. Place on a baking tray lined with baking paper. Brush with the oil and sprinkle with salt and pepper. Bake in the oven at 200°C hot air/gas 7 for approx. 30 minutes, until golden and tender. Leave to cool. Mix the yoghurt with garlic, salt and pepper.

TO SERVE Place the aubergines in a serving dish, spoon the yoghurt over and using a teaspoon spoon over the honey carefully and evenly (it is easier if you hold the spoon 30 cm above the dish). Sprinkle with parsley.

Avocado with rhubarb compote and walnuts

A delicious spring and first course salad.

375 g rhubarb
2 tbsp sugar
50 g walnuts
2 tsp honey
1 large ripe avocado
1 bunch watercress
Salt

DRESSING

1 tbsp olive oil
2 tsp freshly squeezed
   lemon juice
Salt and pepper

Cut the rhubarb into 5 cm pieces, place in an oven-proof dish lined with baking paper, sprinkle with sugar and bake at 175°C hot air/gas 6 for approx. ½ hour, until tender. Toast the nuts in a dry, hot pan until golden, add honey and salt, warm through and leave to cool on a plate. Chop the nuts roughly.

TO SERVE Either as portions in individual bowls or in a serving dish. Place half the watercress at the bottom, then small wedges of avocado, spoon over the dressing, add the rhubarb and finally the rest of the watercress and nuts.

Avocado salad with tomato, oregano and feta cheese

450 g tomatoes
2 ripe avocadoes
50 g red salad onion
150 g cucumber
50 g good quality feta cheese
2 tbsp fresh, chopped oregano
   (or ½ tbsp dried)

DRESSING

2 tsp Dijon mustard
1 tsp white wine vinegar
3 tbsp olive oil
½ tbsp water
1 pinch of sugar
Salt and pepper

Mix the dressing thoroughly. Cut the avocado in half, remove the stone and skin. Cut the avocado diagonally into thin slices. Slice the tomatoes and the onions thinly. Cut the cucumber in half lengthways, remove the seeds and cut into 2 cm thick slices. Cut the feta into thin flakes. Arrange the vegetables in layers, drizzle the dressing in between and on top. Arrange the feta on top and sprinkle with oregano.

Salads with fish

Most salads in this section are suitable either as a first course or for lunch.

PASTA WITH MUSSELS
AND SAFFRON

SALADE NIÇOISE
WITH FRESH TUNA

Pasta with mussels and saffron

The stock is delicious – save a cup of soup for the cook as a treat.

1.5 kg mussels
1 small red chilli
100 g shallots
10 garlic cloves, peeled and
   roughly chopped
1 tbsp olive oil
200 ml white wine
1 large pinch of saffron
   threads
1 bunch parsley
200 g pasta shells
100 ml stock
Freshly squeezed lemon juice,
   to taste
Salt and pepper

Wash and scrub the mussels and discard any that are still open after a light tap on the kitchen sink. Slice the chilli thinly and discard seeds and membranes. Chop the onion and fry in the oil with garlic until clear. Add wine, saffron, chilli, parsley stalks and salt. Leave to simmer for approx. ½ hour under a lid and strain the stock. Discard the parsley stalks and save the rest.
   Add the mussels to the stock and steam under a lid for approx. 4 minutes until the mussels have opened. Remove the mussels from their shells.
   Boil the pasta according to the instructions on the packet, rinse in cold water and leave to drain. Chop the parsley and mix with the pasta, mussels, the onion mixture and the stock. Season to taste, with lemon juice, if necessary.

Salade niçoise with fresh tuna

250 g small new potatoes
2 eggs
250 g fresh tuna fillet
1 tbsp olive oil
100 g small French olives
1 small Romaine lettuce,
   approx. 200 g
½ pot fresh oregano
   (or 2 tsp dried)

DRESSING
2 tsp Dijon mustard
1 garlic clove, peeled and
   finely chopped
1 tbsp lemon-olive oil
   (or 1 tbsp olive oil and 1 tsp
   finely grated lemon zest)
3 tbsp whipping cream
2 tsp freshly squeezed
   lemon juice
1 pinch of sugar
Salt and pepper

Scrub the potatoes and boil with the peel on in lightly salted water until tender. Leave to cool and mix with the dressing. Boil the eggs until hardboiled, 9 minutes. Cut the fish into 4 pieces and fry in the oil over a medium heat for approx. 1½ - 2 minutes on each side. The fish should be pink or slightly red in the centre. Tear the lettuce into mouth-size pieces and rinse in several lots of clean water.
TO SERVE Arrange the salad in portions in individual bowls or on a serving dish. Mix the salad leaves with the potatoes and arrange them at the bottom of the dish, tuna steak on top, then eggs cut into quarters and finally the olives. Garnish with oregano.

Romaine salad with lumpfish roe, croutons and avocado cream

Excellent as a first course arranged in individual portions. If you are cooking for a lot of people you may find a serving dish more practical.

100 g dry white bread
2 tbsp olive oil
1 small Romaine lettuce, approx. 150 g
50 g finely chopped red salad onion
75 g fresh, cleaned lumpfish roe (or salmon roe)

AVOCADO CREAM

1 ripe avocado
1 tsp freshly squeezed lemon juice
150 ml crème fraîche, 9% fat
Pepper

Cut the bread into cubes of approx. ½ x ½ cm. Fry in a pan over a medium heat, until golden, approx. 5 minutes. Leave to cool. Tear the lettuce into mouth-size pieces and rinse in several lots of clean water.

CREAM Mash the avocado and mix with the other ingredients.

TO SERVE Arrange the salad in individual portions or on a serving dish with the lettuce at the bottom. Spoon over the cream, garnish with croutons, spoonfuls of lumpfish roe and red salad onion.

Fish salad in spicy sauce

Ground anise is available from health food shops or Asian greengrocers. Coley goes well with the spicy salad, since it has quite a strong flavour – and on top of that, it is cheap!

4 garlic cloves, peeled and roughly chopped
1 tbsp olive oil
2 tsp ground coriander
½ tsp ground anise seed
3 bay leaves
200 ml white wine
1 tbsp balsamic vinegar
3 tbsp sugar
250 g carrots
150 g leeks
300 g peppers
250 g cod or coley fillet
Salt and pepper
A little broad leaved parsley

Fry the garlic in the oil for a few minutes, add the spices and fry for a little longer. Add wine, vinegar, sugar, salt and pepper and leave to simmer under a lid for approx. 20 minutes. Cut the carrots into broad strips of 5 x ½ x 1 cm, the leeks into 5 cm pieces which you cut again into quarters lengthways, and cut the pepper into thin strips. Add the vegetables to the stock and leave to simmer under a lid for approx. 5 minutes, the vegetables should still be a little crisp. Add more water, if necessary during cooking, but not too much.

Remove the vegetables from the pot and arrange on a serving dish, leave the stock in the pot. Cut the fish into 4 x 2 cm pieces and steam in the stock under a lid for approx. 3 minutes until just cooked through.

TO SERVE Arrange the fish over the vegetables and garnish with chopped broad leaved parsley, serve lukewarm or cold.

ROMAINE SALAD WITH LUMPFISH ROE, CROUTONS AND AVOCADO CREAM

20 g coconut flakes
(or grated coconut)
300 g raw (uncooked)
tiger prawns (or defrosted
from frozen)
1 tbsp neutral tasting oil
2 garlic cloves, peeled and
finely chopped
4 lime leaves
½ red chilli (or to taste)
100 g Iceberg lettuce
100 g pea sprouts
200 g cucumber
Salt

DRESSING

2 tbsp neutral tasting oil
1 tbsp freshly squeezed
lime juice
Salt

Asian prawn cocktail

Coconut flakes are available
from health food shops.
Hijiki – or arame seaweed
that has been left in water to
infuse – may be added.

ASIAN PRAWN COCKTAIL

Toast the coconut flakes in a
dry, hot pan until golden.
Peel the prawns (defrost first,
if necessary) and cut off the
tails. Fry in oil for approx. 2
minutes, until pink all over.
Add the garlic for the last
minute together with the
finely chopped lime leaves,
finely chopped red chilli
(remove seeds and
membranes) and salt. Cut the
lettuce finely, cut the
cucumber into thin strips
(remove the seeds).
TO SERVE Mix all the vegetables
with the dressing. Divide the
mixture between 4 bowls/
glasses, top with the prawns
and finally the coconut flakes.

White fish with seaweed and green beans

This salad can also be made without fish, if so, multiply the portion by 1½ times.

10 g (1 handful) dried
  seaweed (Hijiki or arame)
400 g fresh green beans
250 g fillet of cod or coley
Salt and pepper

DRESSING
2 tbsp neutral tasting oil
1 tsp dark sesame oil
4 tsp freshly squeezed
  lemon juice
1 tbsp tamari
  (or Japanese soy sauce)
1 garlic clove, peeled and
  finely chopped
Salt and pepper

Pour boiling water over the seaweed and leave to infuse for 15 minutes. Trim the beans and steam in a saucepan with a tight fitting lid in a little salted water until almost tender, approx. 3 minutes. Save the bean water. Rinse the beans immediately in cold water. Mix the dressing, add the beans and seaweed and set aside for a minimum of ½ hour.

   Cut the fish into pieces of approx. 3 x 3 cm, sprinkle with salt and pepper and steam carefully under a lid in the bean water for approx. 3 minutes.

TO SERVE Arrange the bean mixture in a serving dish with the fish on top.

Prawn cocktail

Bring out your fine crystal glasses for serving this classic dish. Use organic mayonnaise, if possible.

300 g frozen peeled
  prawns
300 g Iceberg lettuce
4 slices of lemon
  for garnishing

CREAM
300 ml crème fraîche, 9% fat
2 tbsp good quality
  mayonnaise
2 tsp white wine
2 tbsp tomato ketchup
Salt and pepper

Defrost the prawns, and cut the lettuce finely. Mix the cream. Serve in individual portions with the lettuce at the bottom, the prawns on top and finally the cream. Cut 4 slices of approx. ½ cm thick of a lemon, cut a small incision towards the middle of each slice and place a lemon slice on each glass.

PRAWN COCKTAIL

Salads with meat

The meat salads are filling
and are therefore suitable as
individual dishes served
with bread or a green salad.

Thai inspired chicken salad

This salad is also excellent without the chicken, in which case you just add a few more vegetables.

2 chicken breasts, approx. 250 g
1 green chilli (or to taste)
15 lime leaves
2 tbsp neutral tasting oil
2 garlic cloves, peeled and finely chopped
300 g carrots
300 g white cabbage (alternatively summer cabbage or pointed cabbage)
50 g peanuts
1 handful chopped coriander (optional)
Salt

DRESSING

4 tbsp freshly squeezed lime juice
2 tsp muscovado sugar (or soft brown sugar)
Salt

Remove and discard the seeds and membranes from the chilli and cut it into thin strips. Cut the lime leaves into thin strips. Cut the chicken breasts into strips of 1 cm, and fry in the oil with salt, chilli and lime leaves over a medium heat for approx. 4-5 minutes until cooked through. Add garlic for the last minute and stir constantly. Cut the carrots into very thin slices or into julienne strips. Cut the cabbage finely.

Whisk the dressing until the sugar has dissolved. Chop the peanuts.

TO SERVE Mix all the ingredients and garnish with peanuts.

Bulgur salad with chicken

200 g bulgur
300 ml water
40 g (3 tbsp) almonds
3 tbsp olive oil
100 g red salad onion
2 garlic cloves, peeled and finely chopped
1½ tbsp ground coriander
½ tsp ground cinnamon
½ finely grated nutmeg
1 pinch cayenne pepper (or more)
2 chicken breasts, approx. 250 g
400 g squash
50 g (4 tbsp) sultanas
2 tbsp freshly squeezed lemon juice
1 large handful chopped broad leaved parsley
Salt

Pour boiling water over the bulgur, add salt and leave under a lid to absorb all the water, approx. ½ hour. Rinse with cold water and drain. Chop the almonds roughly and toast in a dry, hot pan until golden. Chop the onion finely, fry in the oil for a couple of minutes. Add garlic and spices and fry for a further 5 minutes at medium heat.

Cut the chicken into 1 cm strips and the squash into cubes of approx. 1 x 1 cm. Fry the chicken pieces for 3 minutes. Add the squash, turn up the heat and fry for a further 3 minutes. Add salt and stir the dish constantly during cooking. Mix in all the ingredients and season to taste.

Spinach and lentils with chicken in curry cream

150 g green lentils
3 tbsp neutral tasting oil
1 tbsp freshly squeezed lime juice (or lemon juice)
2 chicken breasts, approx. 250 g
2 tsp curry powder
1 tsp ground ginger
½ tsp ground cardamom
2 garlic cloves, peeled and finely chopped
2 tsp cane sugar
200 ml natural yoghurt
125 g baby spinach
Salt and pepper

Boil the lentils in lightly salted water for approx. 15 minutes until tender. Cool a little and mix in 1 tbsp oil and the lime juice. Cut the chicken breasts into 1 cm strips. Fry the spices at high temperature in 2 tbsp oil for ½ minute, add the chicken strips and fry over a medium heat for approx. 3-4 minutes. Add garlic and sugar and fry for 1 minute. Stir constantly. Leave the chicken pieces to cool, then mix with the lentils and yoghurt, season to taste with salt and pepper. Rinse the spinach thoroughly in several lots of clean water, leave to drain thoroughly.

TO SERVE Arrange the chicken and the lentils on top of the spinach.

Chicken salad with aubergine, tomato and basil cream

300 g aubergine
½ tsp balsamic vinegar
3 tbsp olive oil
2 chicken breasts,
  approx. 250 g
400 g tomatoes on the vine
Salt and pepper

BASIL CREAM
200 ml crème fraîche, 9% fat
1 garlic clove, peeled and
  finely chopped
Zest of ½ lemon
1 pot chopped fresh basil
  (save a little for garnishing)
Salt and pepper

Cut the aubergine into cubes of approx. 1 ½ x 1 ½ cm, mix in 2 tbsp oil, season with salt and pepper and bake in a baking tray lined with baking paper in the oven at 150°C hot air/gas 4 for approx. ½ hour, until tender and golden. but not burnt. Turn during cooking and add the vinegar when cooked.

Cut the chicken breasts into 1 cm strips, and fry in 1 tbsp oil with salt and pepper at medium temperature for approx. 4-5 minutes until cooked through. Stir constantly. Cut the tomatoes into thin slices. Mix the basil cream.

TO SERVE Arrange the tomatoes on a serving dish. Drizzle half the cream over, followed by the chicken and aubergines and garnish with the remaining cream and basil leaves.

Chinese inspired duck breast salad

Anise seed and fennel seeds are available from health food shops and Asian grocers.

1 duck breast, approx 300 g
1 tsp ground anise seed
2 tsp lightly crushed
  fennel seeds
1 pinch ground cinnamon
1 pinch ground cloves
150 g spring onions
150 g cucumber
200 g sugar snaps
100 g baby spinach
1 ½ tbsp rice vinegar or
  white wine vinegar
Salt and lots of black pepper

Cut the fat off the duck breast, cut half into tiny cubes and put the rest in the deep freezer for use later.

Cut the breast into slices of approx. 1 cm. Slice the onion thinly. Cut the cucumber lengthways, scrape out the seeds with a teaspoon and cut into small slices. Cut the sugar snap peas across into strips. Melt the duck fat in the pan and fry the breast and spices at high heat for approx. 6 minutes. Add salt and lots of freshly ground pepper, add the spring onions and fry for 1 minute.

Mix the duck with the vegetables and vinegar and season to taste.

Salads with fruit

Tandoori spice, also called tandoori masala is an Indian spice mixture, which traditionally is used to marinate meat. Grate a little nutmeg over the dish together with the tandoori spice – it tastes delicious.

Orange salad with tandoori spice and mint

The salad goes well with Indian dishes. The orange may be replaced with twice the quantity of mango. If using mango, add a little lemon juice to the olive oil. You can use toasted almonds, pine kernels, walnuts or linseeds instead of pistachio nuts. If the oranges are a little sour, add honey to taste.

1 kg oranges
1 (100 g) red salad onion
60 g salted pistachio nuts
   in their shell
1 tsp tandoori spice
A little olive oil for drizzling
1 small handful fresh
   mint leaves
Salt

Peel the oranges with a sharp knife. Cut into thin slices, remove any seeds and arrange on a serving dish. Peel the onion and cut it into tiny cubes. Remove the shells from the nuts and chop the nuts roughly. Sprinkle the onion over the oranges, sprinkle with tandoori spice, drizzle a little oil over, then a bit of salt, but not too much, since the nuts are salty.

TO SERVE Sprinkle with nuts and chopped mint leaves on top.

Oranges with olives and cream

It sounds strange but it tastes heavenly!

1 kg sweet oranges
50 g Greek Kalamata olives, stones in
3 tbsp whipping cream
Finely chopped red chilli to taste
Salt

Peel the oranges and slice thinly. Remove seeds and arrange the slices on a serving dish. Press lightly on the olives with the palm of your hand, then the stones are easier to remove. Chop the olives roughly. Pour the cream over the orange slices, sprinkle with salt and add olives and chilli. Delicious!

Orange salad with red salad onion and mint

Add more honey if the oranges are a little bitter.

1 kg oranges
200 g red salad onion
Salt
1 small handful fresh
   mint leaves (or broad
   leaved parsley)

2 tbsp olive oil
2 tsp clear honey
½ tsp ground cinnamon
½ tsp ground cumin
1 pinch cayenne pepper

Peel the oranges and slice them thinly. Remove any seeds and arrange the orange slices on a serving dish. Cut the onions into very thin wedges, place in a bowl and pour over boiling water. Leave for a couple of minutes and then drain. Arrange over the oranges and sprinkle with salt. Mix the dressing and pour over the salad. Sprinkle with the mint leaves.

Oranges with fennel

Goes well with duck, lamb and fish. Add more honey if the oranges are a little bitter.

1 kg oranges
1-2 fennel bulbs,
   approx. 200 g
1½ tsp lightly ground
   fennel seeds
1 pinch cayenne pepper
Salt

2 tbsp olive oil
2 tsp clear honey
2 tsp white balsamic vinegar

Peel the oranges and slice them thinly. Remove any seeds and arrange the orange slices on a serving dish. Cut the fennel into very thin slices, save the top, (optional). Mix the dressing and drizzle over the salad. Grind the fennel seeds lightly in a mortar or electric coffee grinder. Sprinkle over the salad with cayenne pepper and salt. Garnish with chopped fennel top.

Brunch salad

This simple salad is delicious for a breakfast or brunch buffet.

5 red grapefruits
50 g sunflower seeds
1 tbsp sugar
Salt

Toast the sunflower seeds in a dry, hot pan until almost golden. Stir during cooking. Add sugar and salt, lower the temperature and stir for a few minutes. Leave to cool. Cut the grapefruits into segments or slices and arrange on a serving dish. Sprinkle with the cooled seeds.

Cucumber and mango with toasted Parma ham

This salad goes well with rice and curry dishes.

700 g cucumber
250 g mango (or fresh
   pineapple or melon)
100 g red salad onion
70 g sliced Parma ham
1 tbsp white balsamic vinegar
Salt and pepper

Peel the cucumbers, cut them lengthways and remove the seeds with a teaspoon. Cut into thin slices. Cut the mango into quarters towards the stone, discard the stone, remove the peel and chop the flesh roughly. Cut the onion into very thin slices. Fry the ham in a pan at high temperature for a few minutes each side, until golden and crisp. Leave to drain on kitchen towel and chop roughly. Mix all the ingredients and season to taste.

Watermelon with feta cheese and parsley

This is a variation on the classic watermelon and feta cheese recipe. Use a good quality feta cheese. Think of this salad as an alternative to the ubiquitous tomato and mozzarella salad.

It is delicious in the summer when the melons are in season. You can use any sort of melon, but the watermelon looks very attractive.

30 g pumpkin seeds (optional)
900 g watermelon
70 g red salad onion
100 g feta cheese
2 handfuls broad
   leaved parsley
1½ tbsp red wine vinegar
Salt and pepper

Toast the seeds in a dry, hot pan. Remove the skin from the melon and cut the flesh into mouth-size pieces. Cut the onion into thin rings and the cheese into thin flakes. Mix all the ingredients, except for the cheese and the seeds. Arrange on a serving dish, place the cheese on top and garnish with the seeds.

Dips and salsas

Dips and salsas are excellent substitutes for sauces with your dinner, served with lots of bread and green salad. They also make delicious snacks served with bread.

Avocado and bean salsa

300 g fresh green beans
2 garlic cloves, peeled and
  finely chopped
2 tbsp white wine vinegar
3 tbsp chopped fresh tarragon
3 small ripe avocadoes
Salt and pepper

Trim the beans and steam in a saucepan with a tight fitting lid in slightly salted water until almost tender, approx. 3 minutes. Rinse immediately in cold water and cut them finely across. Mix all the ingredients, except for the avocado. Cut the avocado into small cubes and mix in carefully. Season the salad to taste.

AVOCADO AND BEAN SALSA

PEPERONATA CREAM, SEE PAGE 122

SPINACH AND AVOCADO TZATZIKI, SEE PAGE 116

CELERIAC SKORDALIA, SEE PAGE 119

Tina's tzatziki

This is a super simple tzatziki, which is delicious with other salads as a side dish with lamb for example.

250 g cherry tomatoes
300 g cucumber
300 g Greek yoghurt 10% fat
3 garlic cloves, peeled and
    crushed
1 large handful chopped broad
    leaved parsley (or mint)
Salt and pepper

Cut the tomatoes into quarters. Cut the cucumber lengthways, remove the seeds with a teaspoon and cut into small cubes. Mix with the other ingredients and season to taste.

Spinach and avocado tzatziki

See photo page 115.
This tzatziki can also be made without the avocado.

300 g baby spinach
1 ripe avocado
300 g Greek yoghurt 10% fat
2 garlic cloves, peeled and
    crushed
Salt and pepper

Steam the spinach in a saucepan without water, drain, leave to cool and squeeze out any remaining liquid. Chop the spinach roughly. Mash the avocado and mix with the yoghurt. Mix with the other ingredients and season to taste.

Melon tzatziki

This is a sweet, but fresh dip which is excellent as the soothing element in hot dishes.

1 kg sweet ripe melon,
    e.g honeydew, Galia
    or cantaloupe
300 g Greek yoghurt 10% fat
1 garlic clove, peeled and
    crushed
1 tsp freshly squeezed
    lemon juice
2 tbsp chopped fresh mint
Salt and pepper

Peel the melon, remove the seeds and cut the melon into tiny cubes. Mix with the other ingredients and season to taste.

Pea and mint tzatziki

1 kg green peas in their pod
200 g Greek yoghurt 10% fat
6 tbsp natural yoghurt
2-3 tbsp chopped fresh mint
1 tsp freshly squeezed
    lemon juice
2 garlic cloves, peeled and
    crushed
Salt and pepper

Pod the peas and chop half of the pods roughly in a food processor. Mix with the rest of the peas and the other ingredients. Season to taste.

Spring tzatziki

Serve for example with fried chicken, fish, lamb and new potatoes. Or as part of a spring or summer buffet. You can turbo chop the radishes by putting them in a food processor for 2 seconds.

1 bunch (approx 125 g)
    radishes
1 (approx 300 g) cucumber
1 small bunch dill
400 g Greek yoghurt 10% fat
2 garlic cloves, peeled and
    crushed
1 tsp freshly squeezed
    lemon juice
A little olive oil for serving
Salt and pepper

Remove the top of the radishes and cut into small cubes. Cut the cucumber lengthways, remove the seeds with a teaspoon and cut it into small cubes. Chop the dill roughly. Save a little of the cucumber, dill and radishes for garnishing. Mix cucumber, radishes, yoghurt, garlic, half the dill, salt and pepper and season to taste. Arrange in a bowl, garnish with cucumber, radishes and dill. Drizzle with oil.

SPRING TZATZIKI

Crunchy Thai salsa

The salad goes well with Thai dishes, or you can serve it with poultry and pork dishes to give them an extra kick. Fish sauce is used instead of salt and as a flavour enhancer in Thai dishes. It tastes better than it smells, so please, do not be put off. Sprinkle 30 g roughly chopped and toasted, salted peanuts over the salsa before serving.

1 (approx 300 g) cucumber
150 g sugar snaps
1 bunch (approx 125 g) radishes
½-1 bunch (2-4) spring onions
1 handful fresh coriander leaves
1 handful basil leaves, Thai basil, if available

DRESSING
½-1 red chilli
1 garlic clove, peeled and crushed
1 tbsp fish sauce
2 tbsp freshly squeezed lime juice
2 tbsp maple syrup

DRESSING Remove seeds and membranes from the chilli and chop the chilli finely. Mix with garlic, fish sauce, lime juice and maple syrup.

Cut the cucumber lengthways, scrape out the seeds with a teaspoon and cut it into small slices. Chop the sugar snap peas in thin slices diagonally across. Remove the top and slice the radishes thinly. Discard the discoloured top and bottom from the onions and slice them thinly. Rinse and dry the herbs.

TO SERVE Chop the herbs roughly, mix with the vegetables and dressing and season the salad to taste.

COARSE THAI SALSA

Celeriac skordalia

This is a variation on the classic Greek potato-based garlic cream. The garlic cream is mild because the garlic cloves have been boiled. It is delicious with meat, fish and poultry served with a green salad and bread. See photo page 115.

500 g celeriac
250 g potatoes
10 garlic cloves, peeled
  and roughly chopped
200 g Greek yoghurt 10% fat
2 tsp dried oregano
Salt and pepper
Olive oil for garnishing

Peel the potatoes and celeriac, cut into smaller pieces and boil with the garlic in unsalted water until all the vegetables are tender. Drain saving 100 ml of the water and leave the vegetables to cool. Mash the vegetables, and mix with the other ingredients including the water. Take care not to stir too much, or the cream will become tough.

Season to taste and spoon the cream into a dish.
TO SERVE Drizzle with a good quality olive oil.

Spinach hummus

150 g dried chick peas
2 bay leaves and 2 garlic
   cloves, peeled for boiling
200 g frozen spinach,
   whole leaves
3 tbsp tahini
Approx. 4 tbsp water
2 garlic cloves crushed
2-3 tsp Garam masala
   (or curry powder)
Cayenne pepper to taste
Approx. 3 tbsp lemon juice
1-2 tbsp sesame seeds,
   for garnishing
Salt

Soak the chick peas in water
overnight. At the same time
take the spinach out of the
freezer, put it in a small bowl
and leave in the fridge.
Rinse the chick peas and boil
in fresh water with bay leaves
and a few garlic cloves for
approx. 1 hour until tender
and soft. Drain the water
and discard.

Put chick peas, spinach
including any liquid, tahini,
water, garlic and spices in a
food processor and blend to a
uniform paste, if necessary,
several steps at a time. Season
to taste with lemon juice and
salt.

Arrange in a bowl and
sprinkle with sesame seeds,
which have been toasted in
a dry, hot pan.

Peperonata cream

This simple dip is delicious and can easily be kept for a couple of days in the fridge. Make a large portion. Without cayenne pepper this dish is super for children. The cream is also delicious as a spread in sandwiches and burgers. See photo page 115.

1 kg red peppers
1 tbsp olive oil
100 ml Greek yoghurt 10% fat
1 tsp balsamic vinegar
1 generous pinch of
    cayenne pepper
Salt and pepper

Cut the peppers into halves, remove the seeds, but leave the skin on and bake them brushed with oil in the oven in a baking tray lined with baking paper at 175°C hot air/ gas 6 for approx. 45 minutes, until golden and tender. Turn the vegetables once during cooking. Blend in a food processor until a uniform paste, mix with the other ingredients and season to taste.

Green olive and almond tapenade

Tapenade is a French olive purée. This is a Greek inspired variation which is delicious on toast, served with a green salad or soup.

120 g green olives, stones out
50 g almonds
2 garlic cloves crushed
2 tbsp olive oil
Salt and pepper

Chop the almonds roughly and toast in a dry, hot pan. Blend with the olives, oil and garlic to a uniform paste. Season to taste.

Red pepper and feta dip

The better quality raw materials you use, the better the result. Buy a soft, good quality feta cheese with character from your local deli or well stocked supermarket.

200 g feta cheese (drained
    weight)
200 ml natural yoghurt
1 red pepper, approx. 150 g
1 tsp paprika
1 generous pinch of
    cayenne pepper

Blend the feta cheese with a little yoghurt in a food processor or blender, add the rest of the yoghurt and blend until the paste is uniform and slightly grainy (looks like cottage cheese). Cut the pepper into tiny cubes, mix with the cheese, add the other ingredients and season to taste.

Avocado and lime salsa

300 g cucumber
70 g spring onions
10 lime leaves
1 garlic clove, peeled and
   finely chopped
2 tbsp freshly squeezed
   lime juice
1 small handful roughly
   chopped fresh coriander
3 small ripe avocadoes
Salt and pepper

Cut the cucumber lengthways,
remove the seeds with a
teaspoon and cut the
cucumber into small cubes.
Cut the spring onion into tiny
pieces and chop the lime
leaves finely. Mix all the
ingredients except for the
avocado. Cut the avocado into
small cubes and mix it
carefully with the salad.
Season to taste.

Avocado, sweetcorn and tomato salsa

2 corn on the cob
500 g tomatoes on the vine
50 g red salad onion
2 garlic cloves, peeled and
   finely chopped
1½ tbsp freshly squeezed
   lime juice
½ tsp ground anise seed
1 tsp ground coriander
1 generous pinch
   cayenne pepper or chopped
   fresh chilli
2 ripe avocadoes
Salt

Cut the corn cobs into halves
and boil them in slightly
salted water until tender,
approx. 10 minutes. Leave to
cool and cut the kernels off
the cobs. Cut the tomatoes into
tiny cubes and the onion into
even smaller cubes. Mix all the
ingredients except for the
avocado. Cut the avocado into
small cubes and mix it
carefully with the salad.
Season the salsa to taste.

Dressings, creams and pestos

Why buy it in bottle when it is so easy to make your own dressing? Home-made dressings are free from additives and they have a natural taste, not synthetic. Keep all these ingredients in the cupboard for superb dressings:

JAPANESE SOY SAUCE

WINE VINEGAR

OLIVE OIL

KETCHUP

CLEAR HONEY

MAPLE SYRUP

ORGANIC MAYONNAISE

JAPANESE SOY SAUCE

LEMON OLIVE OIL

CHINESE
SOY SAUCE

APPLE CIDER
VINEGAR

BALSAMIC VINE-
GAR

TAHINI PASTE

PEANUT BUTTER

NATURAL
YOGHURT

MISO LIGHT

Creative creams and brilliant dressings

When you are short of time during the week, use the vegetables you already have in the fridge and give your salad a lift with one of the following dressings. Sweet and sour should be adjusted to the vegetables you are using. A salad with sweet carrots or baked root vegetables may need a little more lemon juice or vinegar in the dressing.

Is it a cream or dressing? We have chosen to call dressings containing sour milk products 'creams' and the other types 'dressings' but it does not really matter what you call them. If the dressing contains milk products it will keep for a couple of days in the fridge, if not, it will keep for weeks in an airtight container/bottle. Remember to use clean spoons every time you dish up from the container/bottle. Do not whisk crème fraîche with 18% and 9% fat too vigorously it will make them too runny.

Raspberry vinaigrette

Goes well with green salads and salads with poultry and meat.

100 g raspberries (fresh
    or frozen)
1 tsp white wine vinegar
    (or raspberry vinegar
    or other vinegar)
2 tbsp neutral tasting oil
1 tbsp water, if necessary
½ tsp sugar
Salt and pepper

Defrost frozen berries, preferably overnight in the fridge, as they will lose less juice. Or use frozen berries and add water instead of the juice from the defrosted berries. Blend all the ingredients in a food processor or blender with the rest of the ingredients including the juice from the berries. Season to taste.

If possible defrost frozen berries ½ hour before blending.

Mustard dressing with herbs

Suitable for all kinds of beans, potatoes, green salads, salads with asparagus and avocado.

1-2 tbsp olive oil or neutral
    tasting oil
1 tsp white wine vinegar
2 tsp Dijon mustard
Approx. 2 tsp water
½ tsp herbes de Provence
    (optional)
1 pinch of sugar
Salt and pepper

Whisk all the ingredients and season to taste.

Chinese sweet and sour dressing

Suitable for noodle salads, raw salads and salads with fish and shellfish. Goes well with Chinese dishes.

2 tbsp tomato ketchup
4 tsp white wine vinegar
1 tbsp muscovado sugar
    (or soft brown sugar)
1 garlic clove, peeled
    and finely chopped
1 tbsp finely grated
    fresh ginger
½ tsp ground anise seed
2 tbsp neutral tasting oil
Salt and pepper

Mix the ingredients thoroughly, except for the oil until the sugar has dissolved. Add the oil and season to taste.

All recipes are for approx. 4-6 people or 1 kg unprepared vegetables (except the green salads) unless otherwise indicated, but the quantity of dressing is always dependent on the type of vegetable you are using.

Creamy lemon dressing

The dressing for the classic salad. Tastes delicious with green salads, especially with lettuce during the summer season.

5 tbsp whipping cream
4 tsp freshly squeezed
   lemon juice
1½ tsp sugar
Salt and pepper

Shake the dressing in a jam jar and pour over the salad just before serving.

Miso dressings

Taste delicious with raw vegetables, as a dip for vegetable sticks, and with quinoa, buckwheat noodles, rice and bean salads.

Miso dressing with lime and garlic

4 tbsp miso, light or dark
Zest of 1 organic lime
2 tbsp freshly squeezed
   lime juice
1 garlic clove, peeled and
   crushed
1½ tbsp maple syrup
   (or clear honey)
A little water, if necessary

Whisk all the ingredients and season the dressing to taste. Add a little water, if the dressing is too thick.

Miso dressing with ginger and wasabi

3 tbsp miso, light or dark
2 tsp peeled, freshly
   grated ginger
1 garlic clove, peeled and
   crushed
1 tsp wasabi from tube
1 tbsp apple cider vinegar
3 tbsp water

Whisk all the ingredients and season the dressing to taste.

Peanut cream

Tastes delicious with raw vegetables, as a dip for vegetable sticks, and with quinoa, buckwheat noodles, rice and bean salads.

3 tbsp crunchy peanut butter
1 garlic clove, peeled and
  crushed
2 tbsp freshly squeezed
  lime juice (or lemon juice)
2 tbsp soy sauce
2 tsp maple syrup
  (or clear honey)
½ tsp ground cumin (optional)
Approx. 1 tsp water
Cayenne pepper

Whisk all the ingredients for the cream and season to taste. It should be sweet-sour-light-strong.

Tahini dressing

Tastes delicious with green salads, raw vegetables, baked vegetables, and with potato, quinoa, bulgur and bean salads. Delicious with chopped herbs sprinkled on top.

3 tbsp tahini
1 garlic clove, peeled and
  crushed
4 tbsp freshly squeezed
  lemon juice
3-4 tbsp water
Cayenne pepper to taste
Salt

Whisk tahini with garlic, and add lemon juice a little at a time. At first it becomes thick, then thinner. Add water if the consistency is like whipping cream. Add salt and cayenne pepper to taste.

Yoghurt dressing with olive oil

Suitable for green salads and raw vegetables. Add ground cumin, curry powder, tandoori spice, paprika, smoked paprika or fresh herbs to taste.

200 ml natural yoghurt with
  3.5% fat
1 tbsp good olive oil
1 garlic clove, peeled and
  crushed
Salt and pepper

Mix all the ingredients and season the dressing to taste.

Horseradish cream

Suitable for salads with potatoes, beetroot, tomatoes and baked root vegetables.

200 ml crème fraîche, 9% fat
2 tbsp whole, finely grated
  horseradish
2½ tsp white wine vinegar
2 tsp sugar
Salt and pepper

Mix all the ingredients and season the cream to taste.

Sonja's Thousand Island dressing

Goes well with prawn cocktail and with grilled fish. Give it a bit of oomph with a little chilli sauce or cayenne pepper.

200 ml crème fraîche, 9% fat
1½ tbsp tomato ketchup
1 tsp freshly squeezed
   lemon juice
½ tbsp sherry or white wine
Salt and pepper

Mix all the ingredients and season the dressing to taste.

Tina's little pink

This is the home-made version of the Thousand Island dressing you buy in a bottle. When the kids demand shop bought salad dressing, try this one.

200 ml crème fraîche, 9% fat
   or Greek yoghurt 10% fat
1 garlic clove, peeled and
   crushed
Approx. 5 tbsp ketchup
Salt and pepper

Mix all the ingredients and season the dressing to taste.

Pesto

Most people have heard of pesto. This one differs from the usual one with the lemon juice, which we think adds freshness to the salads. Goes well with pasta salads, potatoes, beans, tomatoes, aubergines and most vegetables.

100 ml olive oil
4 tsp lemon juice
15 g (approx 1½ tbsp)
   pine kernels
2 tbsp finely grated Parmesan
2 handfuls basil leaves
1- 2 garlic cloves, peeled and
   crushed
Salt and pepper

Blend all the ingredients to a uniform paste. How coarse is a matter of taste.
   Go easy on the salt since the Parmesan cheese is salty.

Coarse mint hazelnut pesto

Goes well with pasta, beans, bulgur, raw vegetables and much more.

50 g hazelnuts
2 tbsp olive oil
3 tbsp finely chopped
   fresh mint
1 garlic clove, peeled and
   finely chopped
2 tsp freshly squeezed
   lemon juice
1 generous pinch of
   cayenne pepper
Salt

Toast the hazelnuts in a dry, hot pan and chop them roughly. Mix all the ingredients and season to taste.

Olive oil balsamic vinegar dressing

The best quality oil and vinegar should be used for this recipe. Goes well with green salads, tomato salads, raw vegetables, potato salads etc. Chopped fresh herbs, or dried, can be added for extra flavour.

2 tbsp olive oil
2 tsp balsamic vinegar
½ tsp sugar (optional)
Salt and pepper

Whisk all the ingredients and season to taste.

Summer buffet

SPELT BREAD

CHEESE

POTATOES WITH LEMON OLIVE OIL, PINE
KERNELS AND ROCKET SALAD

CARPACCIO OF
FILLET OF BEEF

TOMATOES WITH FRIED PEPPERS
AND MOZZARELLA

Brilliant buffets

Buffets are wonderful for parties. Everything can be prepared in advance, before the guests arrive. The dishes are inviting and tempting, and the guests look after themselves, so the host can participate in the party without having to keep an eye on things. The guests are not forced to sit in the same seat during the entire meal, since they have to keep getting up to help themselves to the food.

MERINGUE CAKE WITH WHIPPED CREAM, RED CURRANTS AND WHITE CHOCOLATE

MEAT ON SKEWERS

PEA AND MINT TZATZIKI

MUSSELS STEAMED IN WHITE WINE

Fish dishes for buffets

Fish on skewers and fish tartare are both excellent served as a first course as individual portions. The skewers provide 8 portions as a first course, the tartares 5 portions as a first course, and the mussels 6 portions.

Mussels steamed in white wine

SERVES 8-10

3 kg mussels
200 g shallots
10 garlic cloves, peeled and
    roughly chopped
2 tbsp olive oil
400 ml white wine
Salt and pepper
Chopped broad leaved
    parsley may be added
    for garnishing

Wash and scrub the mussels and discard any that are still open after a light tap on the kitchen sink. Chop the onion and fry it in the oil with garlic until clear. Add wine, pepper and salt. Leave to simmer for approx. ½ hour under a lid. Add the mussels to the stock and steam under a lid for approx. 4 minutes until opened. Turn over a few times during cooking. Serve in a large bowl or in individual small bowls, hot or lukewarm sprinkled with chopped broad leaved parsley.

Salmon tartare with wasabi

Wasabi is Japanese horseradish which is used for sushi. It is available as a powder which is mixed to a paste with a little water or as a finished paste in tubes. Available from sushi bars, Asian supermarkets and very well stocked supermarkets. Use freshly grated horseradish instead, if necessary.

SERVES 8

400 g skinless salmon fillets
    (450 g with skin)
1-2 tsp wasabi paste
    (or to taste)
Salt
Lettuce leaves (optional)

Remove the skin from the salmon, and any bones, if necessary. Cut into tiny cubes. Mix with the other ingredients and season to taste. Form the tartare into egg shapes, using a dessert spoon and arrange the 'eggs' on a serving dish on lettuce leaves.

The quantities are for buffets with 3 kinds of meat or fish. If the fish dishes are served as a main course or for lunch, they only provide half the number of servings.

WHOLE OVEN BAKED SALMON

1. RAW SALMON ready for baking (the lemon slices on top are for the benefit of the photographer).

2. BAKED SALMON just out of the oven.

3. REMOVE THE SKIN by cutting along the back bone and lifting the skin with a knife.

Whole oven baked salmon

SERVES 20

1 salmon of 2.8-3 kg
Herbs, for example dill,
    parsley, mint
2 organic lemons
Fennel seeds (optional)
Salt and pepper

Place the salmon in a baking tray lined with baking paper. Stuff it with herbs and slices of lemon. Sprinkle with salt and pepper and fennel seeds. Bake in the oven for approx. 1 hour at 175°C hot air/gas 6, until just cooked through. Check at the back bone if the flesh is raw. If it is still raw, bake the salmon for a little longer.

6. THE OTHER SIDE is now ready to serve.

4. SERVE THE SALMON like this on the buffet. Cut down along the middle bone and indicate the portions with a cross section. Garnish with sprigs of dill for example.

5. WHEN THE UPPER SIDE is finished, remove the head and bones: Get hold of the head and lift it down towards the tail. Remove the biggest remaining bones.

Salmon tartare with herbs

SERVES 8

400 g skinless salmon fillets
   (450 g with skin)
4 tbsp chopped dill
4 tbsp finely chopped chives
2 tsp Dijon mustard
4 tsp freshly squeezed
   lemon juice
Salt and pepper
Lettuce leaves for garnishing

Remove the skin from the salmon, and any bones, if necessary. Cut the salmon into tiny cubes. Mix with the other ingredients and season to taste. Form the tartare into egg shapes using a spoon and arrange the 'eggs' on a bed of lettuce leaves on a serving dish.

White fish tartare with lime and coriander

SERVES 8

400 g whole fresh pollack
   or fillet of cod
40 g red salad onion
1 large handful chopped
   fresh coriander
1 tsp finely chopped green
   chilli (or to taste)
2 tbsp lime juice
2 tbsp olive oil
Salt
Lettuce leaves

Remove any fish bones. Cut the fish and onion into tiny cubes. Mix with the other ingredients and season to taste. Form the tartare into egg shapes, using a spoon and arrange the 'eggs' on a bed of lettuce leaves in a serving dish.

White fish tartare with dill and Dijon mustard

SERVES 8

400 g whole fresh pollack
   or fillet of cod
4 tbsp chopped dill
4 tbsp finely chopped chives
2 tsp Dijon mustard
2 tbsp olive oil
2 tbsp freshly squeezed
   lemon juice
Salt and pepper
Lettuce leaves

Remove any fish bones. Cut the fish into tiny cubes. Mix with the other ingredients and season to taste. Form the tartare into egg shapes, using a spoon and arrange the 'eggs' on a bed of lettuce leaves in a serving dish.

CEVICHE À LA JAPAN,
SEE PAGE 138

CEVICHE WITH POMEGRANATE, SEE PAGE 138

Ceviche

Ceviche is a South American salad where the fresh raw fish is 'cooked' by the acid in the lemon juice. You can use any kind of white fish. Serve the salad as a first course or as a dish for a buffet.

Ceviche à la Japan

This is a Japanese inspired version. Read about the seaweed on page 12. See photo page 136.

2 handfuls (20 g) dried
   wakame or arame seaweed
400 g pollack (or cod)
1 green chilli (or to taste)
150 ml freshly squeezed
   lime juice from approx.
   5 limes (or lemon juice)
1 ½ tsp dark sesame oil
Salt
Finely chopped chives
   to garnish

Pour boiling water over the seaweed and leave to infuse for 15 minutes. Drain the water and discard.

Cut the fish into cubes of no more than 1 x 1 cm. Remove seeds and membranes from the chilli and chop it finely. Mix fish and seaweed with chilli, lime juice, sesame oil and salt in a small serving dish. Leave in the fridge for at least 3 hours until the fish has turned white.

TO SERVE Season the ceviche to taste and garnish with chives.

Ceviche with pomegranate

See photo page 137.

400 g fresh fillet of halibut
½ red chilli (or to taste)
150 ml freshly squeezed
   lime juice from approx.
   5 limes (or lemon juice)
3 tbsp finely chopped red
   salad onion
1 garlic clove, peeled and
   crushed
Seeds from ½ pomegranate
Fresh coriander for
   garnishing
Salt

Cut the fish into cubes of no more than 1 x 1 cm. Remove seeds and membranes from the chilli and chop it finely. Mix fish and chilli with lime juice, onion, garlic and salt in a small bowl. Leave in the fridge for at least 3 hours until the fish has turned white. Cut the pomegranate into quarters and remove the seeds. Discard the white bitter membranes.

TO SERVE Season the ceviche to taste and garnish with the pomegranate seeds and roughly chopped coriander.

Fish on skewers

Anything on skewers always creates excitement, maybe it is our past as hunter/gatherers that still affects us? The chopped herbs may be parsley, dill or a mixture of the two. Parsley-basil goes well with salmon. A mixture of herbs and zest of lemon also goes well together. Buy a stock of wooden skewers while the shops are selling them during the barbecue season.

SERVES 8-10 (16 SKEWERS)

650 g firm skinless fish fillets
    (700 g with skin), for
    example pollack, monkfish,
    salmon, halibut or tuna
Olive oil
Salt and pepper
Freshly squeezed lemon juice
Chopped herbs

Remove any skin and bones and cut the fillets into cubes of approx. 2 x 3 cm. Place the fish cubes on skewers, 3-4 on each. Brush with oil, sprinkle with salt and pepper and bake in the oven at 175°C hot air/gas 6 for approx. 7 minutes (9 minutes for monkfish) until the fish is just cooked through.
TO SERVE Serve hot or luke-warm. Arrange on serving dishes, drizzle with lemon juice and sprinkle with herbs. Alternatively, drizzle with one of the sauces, or serve the sauce separately in a bowl next to the skewers.

VARIATION 1
Tahini sauce for fish skewers

The fish skewers are prepared as in the previous recipe. Instead of herbs they are served with tahini sauce (sesame seed paste) which is delicious with fish.

4 tbsp tahini
200 ml natural yoghurt
1½ tbsp lemon juice
2 garlic cloves, peeled and
    finely chopped
1 pinch cayenne pepper
Salt
Chopped broad leaved parsley
    to sprinkle on top

Mix all the ingredients and season the sauce to taste. Leave the skewers to cool, arrange them on a serving dish, drizzle the sauce on top and sprinkle with parsley. Alternatively, sprinkle the skewers with herbs and serve the sauce in a bowl with the skewers.

VARIATION 2
Satay sauce for fish skewers

The fish skewers are prepared as described in fish on skewers, but the herbs are replaced by a peanut butter sauce. This is best served with a strong tasting fish such as salmon, tuna and pollack. It also tastes delicious as a sauce served with small baked potatoes or raw vegetable sticks.

50 g onions
2 garlic cloves, peeled and
    finely chopped
1 tbsp neutral tasting oil
2 tsp ground cumin
5 lime leaves
1 tsp muscovado sugar
    (or soft brown sugar)
8 tbsp peanut butter
200 ml (½ tin) coconut milk
3 tbsp freshly squeezed
    lemon juice
250 ml water
1 tsp Sambal oelek (or other
    chilli of your choice)
Salt

Chop the onion and fry for a couple of minutes in the oil with garlic, cumin and finely chopped lime leaves over a medium heat. Add the other ingredients (whisk the coconut milk in a bowl before measuring), mix thoroughly and leave the sauce to simmer under a lid for at least ½ hour while continuing to stir. Add a little more water during cooking, if necessary, the consistency should be like a thick sauce. Season to taste.

Meat dishes for buffets

Many of the salads in our book have a lot of character and are spicy in themselves. They will often be best suited to neutral meat, such as a fried topside/silverside, roast leg of lamb, or turkey breast – or several kinds of sliced meat. Here are a few guidelines and roasting times for the oven. Sprinkle with salt and pepper before roasting and remember to leave the meat to rest under cover after cooking has finished.

The quantities are for buffets with 3 kinds of meat or fish. If the meat dishes are served as a main course or for lunch, they only provide half the number of servings indicated.

VEAL TOPSIDE/SILVERSIDE
Roast 1 veal silverside/topside
of approx. 1 kg for 15 minutes
at 200°C hot air/gas 7 and
25 minutes at 175°C hot air/
gas 6. Serves 10

BEEF TOPSIDE/SILVERSIDE
Roast 1 beef silverside/topside
of approx. 1.1–1.2 kg for
15 minutes at 200°C hot air/
gas 7 and 35 minutes at
175°C hot air/gas 6. Serves
approx. 10 people.

CARVING SILVERSIDE/TOPSIDE

LEG OF LAMB Roast 1 leg of lamb
of approx. 1½ kg for
1½ hours at 175°C hot air/
gas 6. Serves 8-10 people.

LAMB SHANK Roast a lamb shank
of approx. 1.2 kg for
1 hour and 20 minutes at
175°C hot air/gas 6. Serves
approx. 10 people.

TURKEY BREAST Brown 1 turkey
breast of approx. 1 kg in
the pan, and roast in the oven
at 175°C hot air/gas 6 for
approx. 50 minutes. Serves
approx. 10 people.

DUCK BREAST Roast 5 duck
breasts in the oven for
25 minutes at 195°C hot air/
gas 8. Serves approx.
10 people.

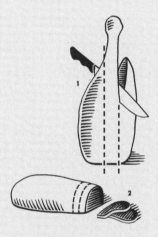

CARVING LEG OF LAMB

Roast turkey breast with herbs and white wine

SERVES APPROX.10

600 g vegetables, for example
  leeks, red salad onion
  and carrots
1 kg turkey breast
3 tbsp olive oil
300 ml white wine
5 garlic cloves, peeled and
  roughly chopped
1 large handful roughly
  chopped herbs, for example
  sage, thyme and rosemary
Salt and pepper

Clean the vegetables and cut
them roughly. Brown the
breast on both sides in oil in a
pan, add salt and pepper.
Deglaze the pan with white
wine. Place vegetables, garlic
and herbs at the bottom of an
ovenproof dish and sprinkle
with salt and pepper. Add the
turkey and pour over white
wine. Roast in the oven at
175°C hot air/gas 6 for 50
minutes. Leave the meat to
rest for ½ hour under cover.
Carve the breast into thin
slices and serve on a dish with
the herbs.

Lamb shank with garam masala

Garam masala is an Indian/
Pakistani spice mixture
similar to curry powder.
Available from Asian grocers.

SERVES APPROX.10 PEOPLE

1 boned lamb shank
  of approx.1.2 kg
3 cloves of garlic
Garam masala
Neutral tasting oil
Salt

Cut the garlic into 3-4 pieces.
Make a cut in the meat and
push in the garlic pieces.
Rub the meat with garam
masala, salt and pepper,
place in an ovenproof dish
and drizzle a little oil over.
Roast in the oven at 175°C hot
air/gas 6 for 1 hour and 20
minutes. Leave the meat to
rest for ½ hour under cover
and carve it into thin slices.

Carpaccio of fillet of beef

SERVES 20

750 g fillet of beef or veal
2 tbsp olive oil for frying and
  a little more for drizzling
100 g whole Parmesan cheese
Salt and pepper
Rocket or radicchio

Remove the fat and tendons
from the fillet using a sharp
knife. Brown at high
temperature in oil all over.
Season with salt and pepper,
leave to cool slightly, then
wrap in plastic film and place
in the freezer for 3-4 hours
until it is semi frozen, so you
can slice it very thinly. You
can also freeze it completely
and then take it out of the
freezer 3-4 hours before
slicing it.

ONE HOUR BEFORE SERVING

Cut the fillet in 1 mm thin
slices and arrange on a
serving dish on a bed of
rocket or radicchio. Drizzle
with the oil, sprinkle with salt
and pepper and Parmesan
shavings.

Meatballs with cranberries and pistachio nuts

SERVES 6-8
APPROX.25 SMALL MEATBALLS

500 g minced veal and pork
(or turkey/chicken)
70 g red salad onion
50 g salted pistachio nuts
in their shell
40 g (4 tbsp) dried cranberries
½ pot freshly chopped thyme
(or 2 tsp dried)
1 egg
100 ml milk
2 tbsp breadcrumbs
1 tsp salt
Pepper
Neutral tasting oil for frying

Chop the onion finely.
Remove the shells from the
pistachio nuts and chop the
nuts and cranberries roughly,
then mix with the other
ingredients. Leave the meat
mixture in the fridge for a
minimum of ½ hour.
Shape into small meatballs
using a tablespoon, which you
regularly dip in the fat in the
frying pan. Fry the meatballs
over a medium heat for
approx. 12-15 minutes.

Beef meatballs with ham and sage

SERVES 6-8
APPROX.25 SMALL MEATBALLS

500 g minced beef
100 g boiled smoked ham
(slices from a packet)
3 tbsp chopped fresh sage
(or 1 tbsp dried)
4 garlic cloves, peeled,
finely chopped
1 tbsp zest of organic lemon
1 egg
100 ml water
2 tbsp breadcrumbs
½ tsp salt
Pepper
Neutral tasting oil for frying

Chop the ham finely and mix
with the other ingredients.
Place in the fridge for at least
½ hour. Shape the mixture
into small meatballs using a
tablespoon, which you
continue to dip in the fat in
the frying pan. Fry the
meatballs over a medium heat
for approx.12-15 minutes.

Indian meatballs

SERVES 6-8
APPROX.25 SMALL MEATBALLS

500 g minced beef
(or lamb)
2 garlic cloves, peeled,
finely chopped
2 tbsp breadcrumbs
1 egg
100 ml natural yoghurt
1 tbsp garam masala
(or curry powder)
1 generous pinch of cayenne
pepper
1 tsp salt
Neutral tasting oil for frying

Mix all the ingredients.
Place in the fridge for a
minimum of ½ hour.
Shape into small meatballs
using a tablespoon, which you
continue to dip into the fat in
the frying pan. Fry the
meatballs at medium heat for
approx.12-15 minutes.

Meat on skewers

For this recipe use fresh herbs, if available, they taste better.

SERVES 12
APPROX. 24 SKEWERS

1 kg beef, for example fillet of beef, beef or veal topside/silverside

MARINADE
4 tbsp olive oil
4 tbsp balsamic vinegar
4 tbsp chopped fresh rosemary (or 4 tsp dried)
2 garlic cloves, peeled and finely chopped
2 tsp sugar
Salt and pepper

Remove the fat and tendons, if necessary, and cut the meat into cubes of approx. 3 x 3 cm. Place 4 pieces of meat on the middle of each skewer, brush with the marinade, place in a baking tray lined with baking paper and roast in the oven at 225°C hot air/gas 9 for approx. 5 minutes. Serve hot or lukewarm.

Chicken satay with peanut sauce

These skewers go well with the Asian salads for example with the noodle salads. They can also be served without the sauce.

SERVES APPROX. 10 PEOPLE
(16 SKEWERS)

1 kg chicken fillets, approx. 8 breasts
4 limes (optional)

MARINADE
4 tbsp neutral tasting oil
2 garlic cloves, peeled and finely chopped
1 tbsp ground cumin
2 tbsp ground coriander
2 tsp muscovado sugar (or soft brown sugar)
2 tsp Sambal oelek (or chilli to taste)
Salt

PEANUT SAUCE
75 g onions
3 garlic cloves, peeled and finely chopped
1½ tbsp neutral tasting oil
4 tsp ground cumin
7 lime leaves
1½ tsp muscovado sugar (or soft brown sugar)
12 tbsp peanut butter
1 tin (400 ml) coconut milk
4½ tbsp freshly squeezed lemon juice
Approx. 350 ml water
1½ tsp Sambal oelek (or other chilli of your choice)
Salt

Cut the meat into pieces of approx. 3 x 3 cm. Mix the marinade and add the meat. Leave for a minimum of ½ hour, overnight if possible. Place the meat on skewers, 4 pieces on each.

THE SAUCE Chop the onions and fry in the oil with garlic, cumin and finely chopped lime leaves for a couple of minutes at medium heat. Add the other ingredients, mix well and leave the sauce to simmer under a lid for a minimum of ½ hour, regularly stirring. Add a little more water during cooking, if necessary, the consistency should be like a thick sauce. Season to taste.

TO SERVE Roast the skewers in the oven on a baking tray lined with baking paper at 225°C hot air/gas 9 for 8 minutes. Heat the sauce and serve with the skewers. Cut the limes into quarters and put them on the skewers or serve them with the meat.

CHICKEN SALAD WITH PEANUT SAUCE

Bread and cakes for buffets

No buffet is complete without good bread or a sweet dish to finish off.

For the cakes we use the fruits in season and fresh ingredients.

Cold raised spelt bread

MAKES 1 LARGE LOAF OR APPROX. 30 BUNS

1 litre cold water
25 g yeast
2 tbsp salt
1 tbsp sugar
2 tsp fennel seeds (optional)
300 g coarse spelt flour
(or wholemeal flour)
Approx.1 kg plain white flour

Dissolve the yeast in the water with the sugar and salt.
Mix in the flour and seeds (if using) a little at a time. Knead the dough thoroughly, using an electric mixer if necessary. The dough should be sticky and soft. Leave to rise overnight in the fridge.

Shape into small buns with a spoon and place them close together on a baking tray lined with baking paper. Bake at 175°C hot air/gas 6 for ½ hour. If you form the dough into a loaf, bake for 50-60 minutes at 175°C hot air/gas 6.

Chapatti

**INDIAN FLAT BREAD
MAKES 8**

200 g plain white flour
50 g wholemeal flour
(or coarse spelt flour)
1 tsp salt
1 tbsp neutral tasting oil
Approx.150 ml water

Sift the flour, add the salt, heat the oil in a saucepan and mix with the flour. Add cold water a little at a time until the dough is smooth. Knead for 5 minutes until it is no longer sticky. Leave the dough to rest at room temperature under cling film for 1-2 hours.

Form 8 buns from the dough. Roll them out into flat pancakes (max 3 mm thick) and fry in a little oil (brushed on the frying pan) at low heat for approx. 2-3 minutes each side. They should be baked through and as pale as possible. May be brushed with oil on both sides immediately after cooking.

Pita bread

MAKES 16

600 ml water
50 g yeast
1 tsp sugar
2 tsp salt
2 tbsp olive oil
Approx. 900 g plain white flour

Dissolve the yeast in lukewarm water with the sugar and salt and add the other ingredients. Knead the dough until it is smooth. Leave to rise to double in size, for approx. 1 hour, knead again and divide it into 16 equal pieces. Roll them out ½ cm thick, place on oven trays lined with baking paper and leave to rise again for approx. 15 minutes. Brush with water and bake in a 225°C hot air/gas 9 for 10 minutes, then the pockets are formed automatically.

Meringue cake with whipped cream, redcurrants, and white chocolate

**SUMMER DESSERT
SERVES APPROX. 12**

MERINGUES

4 egg whites
1 tsp vinegar
250 g caster sugar
100 g almonds

FILLING

500 ml whipping cream
300 g redcurrants

100 g white chocolate

Whisk egg whites, vinegar and sugar with an electric whisk for approx. 5 minutes until thick and shiny. Chop the almonds roughly and mix with the egg white mixture. Line a baking tray with baking paper, draw 2 circles approx. 20 cm in diameter on the paper, turn the paper over and sprinkle it lightly with flour. Place the egg white mixture inside the circles. Bake at 135°C hot air/gas 3 for approx. 1 hour and 10 minutes until crisp. Turn off the oven and leave the meringue in the oven with the oven door ajar until they have cooled.

Chop the chocolate, melt in a saucepan at a low temperature and leave to cool a little. Spoon the chocolate in stripes over the meringue.

Whisk the cream until firm and add the cleaned berries.

TO SERVE Assemble the cake starting with a meringue, then the berry cream and another meringue on top.

Apple trifle

This is a variation on the traditional Danish apple cake with whipped cream and the recipe is based on one from our old college textbook. This dessert looks stylish served in glasses – for example café latte glasses or large red wine glasses. If you are cooking for a lot of people, look out for cheap glasses in local cut price shops, go to Ikea or rent the glasses.

APPLE SAUCE

3 kg apples, preferably
  cooking apples
200 ml water or more,
  if necessary
80 g sugar or more,
  if necessary

RYE BREADCRUMBS

400 g dark rye bread,
  without seeds
180-240 g muscovado sugar
1 tbsp ground cinnamon
80 g hazelnuts
100 g good quality
  dark chocolate

600 ml whipping cream

Peel and core the apples, and cut into smaller pieces. Boil under a lid at low temperature until cooked, approx. 15-20 minutes. Stir and mash the apples during cooking and add a little water, if necessary. Add sugar to taste, the sauce should preferably be a little sour.

BREADCRUMBS Grate the rye bread on the coarse side of a vegetable grater. Sprinkle in the muscovado sugar. Add cinnamon and roughly chopped hazelnuts. Put the mixture into a frying pan and warm the breadcrumbs over a medium heat for 1 minute, stirring continuously. Turn down the heat. Leave the breadcrumbs to dry for approx. ½ hour while stirring now and then. Set aside to cool and add the roughly chopped chocolate. Whisk the cream until stiff.

TO SERVE Place sauce and breadcrumbs in layers in individual glasses, 2 layers of each ingredient, starting with the sauce. Finally top with the cream.

Rhubarb layer cake with ginger

3 sponge cakes
100 g macaroons, crushed

SAUCE

750 g rhubarb
200 g sugar
2 tbsp finely grated
  fresh ginger

CREAM

4 pasteurised egg yolks
2 tbsp sugar
250 ml whipping cream
200 g Greek yoghurt 10% fat

COVERING AND GARNISH

50 g good quality milk
  chocolate
50 ml whipping cream
1 tsp butter
Lemon balm

Remove the leaves and any brown bits at the bottom of the rhubarb, cut into 5 cm pieces and boil under a lid with sugar and ginger over a low heat for approx. ½ hour, while stirring all the time.

Mix eggs and sugar until foamy, whisk the cream until stiff, and turn it all carefully into the yoghurt.

Chop the chocolate finely and melt it in a saucepan with cream and butter over a low heat continuing to stir.

Assemble the cake in this order: Start with a sponge cake followed by half the sauce, then half the macaroons and half the cream. Place another sponge cake on top and continue as above. Finish with a sponge cake on top and coat the cake with the covering. The cake may be kept in the fridge for a couple of hours before serving. Garnish with the lemon balm.

Lemon pine kernel cake with whipped cream and lavender

SUMMER DESSERT SERVES APPROX. 8

Semolina is a coarse wheat flour which is available from Asian grocers and well stocked supermarkets. It gives the cake a slightly coarser structure. Dried lavender and blueberry jam is available from health food shops. The cake is brilliant in the summer when you have fresh lavender flowers for garnishing.

CAKE

110 g softened butter
200 g cane sugar
3 eggs
175 g semolina
  (or plain white flour)
50 ml + 50 ml freshly
  squeezed lemon juice
50 g pine kernels
Zest of 1 organic lemon
Icing sugar to garnish

WHIPPED CREAM WITH LAVENDER

2 tsp dried lavender
  (or equal amount of fresh)
1 tbsp blueberry jam
250 ml whipping cream

Fresh lavender flowers,
  if available

Leave the lavender to steep in the jam while the cake is cooking. Toast the pine kernels in a dry, hot pan and leave them to cool. Whisk the butter and sugar thoroughly with an electric whisk, add the eggs, one at a time.

Add 50 ml lemon juice and the other ingredients and whisk quickly. Pour the mixture into a 22-23 cm well greased spring form tin and bake for 40-45 minutes at 150°C hot air/gas 4. Check the middle of the cake with a skewer or fork to see if it is done. If any dough is sticking to the fork or skewer the cake will need a little longer. Leave the cake to cool, prick it with a fork and pour 50 ml lemon juice over.

WHIPPED CREAM Mash the jam with a spoon. Whisk the cream until firm and add the jam.

TO SERVE Dust the cake with icing sugar through a sieve, garnish with fresh lavender flowers, if available, and serve the cake with the whipped cream.

You could also garnish the cakes with edible flowers during the summer season. For example, lavender, daisies, geranium or roses.

Chocolate mousse with fruit in muscovado syrup

A delicious winter dessert. The portions are not particularly big, since this dessert is quite rich. On the other hand it tastes fantastic.

SERVES 8-10

MOUSSE

200 g dark chocolate
100 ml strong coffee
2 pasteurised egg yolks
500 ml whipping cream

FRUITS IN SYRUP

150 g muscovado sugar
150 ml water
½ vanilla pod
1 star anise
½ stick cinnamon
10 g dried apricots
1 green pear (approx. 150 g)

Chop the chocolate and melt it in a saucepan over a low heat. Remove the saucepan from the heat, add coffee and egg yolks, and mix thoroughly. Leave to cool a little. Whip the cream and carefully stir into the chocolate. Arrange in small individual glasses or in a larger glass bowl and leave in the fridge for 3-4 hours.

SYRUP Boil sugar, water and spices in a saucepan without a lid over a low heat for approx. ½ hour, add the apricots and boil for a further 15 minutes. Add the unpeeled pear cut into thin wedges and boil for 15 minutes. Stir during cooking. The consistency should be thick and syrup like. Leave the syrup to cool. If the apricots are very soft from the start they will need less cooking time. The same applies to the pear, if it is very ripe.

TO SERVE Arrange syrup and fruits over the mousse or serve as a side dish in a separate bowl.

All the smaller
buffets are for
8 people

Smaller buffets

The smaller buffets can be served for lunch or dinner.

You could also use them as an inspiration for work place lunches.

For the smaller buffets we either used salads based on different ethnic kitchens or themes, for example 'Her Buffet' with light dishes, 'His buffet' with the heavier dishes and 'Brunch buffet,' where we strongly believe salads should have a place.

You can easily make the buffets on the same day you want to serve them, but we have divided the preparations into two days, if you are short of time on the day. See also the comments for the party buffets on page 160.

Brunch buffet

Arabic buffet

Yoghurt and muesli

1 LITRE

Muesli from the Apple trifle
recipe on page 150,
½ the recipe; use rolled oats
instead of rye bread.

Brunch salad

PAGE 109, 1½ TIMES RECIPE

Watermelon with feta cheese and parsley

PAGE 110, 1½ TIMES RECIPE

Sausages

700 G

Bacon

600 G

Scrambled eggs

MADE FROM 16 EGGS

Spelt bread, butter and cheeses, (optional)

½ – 1 TIMES RECIPE

THE DAY BEFORE

Make the muesli
Toast the nuts for the
brunch salad
Toast the pumpkin seeds
for the watermelon salad
Make the dough for the
spelt bread

ON THE DAY ITSELF

Make the rest

Arabic meatballs

APPROX. 50 SMALL MEATBALLS

1 kg minced beef or lamb
2 eggs
200 g finely grated onion
1 generous pinch dried mint
1½ tsp ground cinnamon
1½ tsp ground cumin
1 tbsp ground allspice
2 handfuls chopped parsley
1 generous pinch of
cayenne pepper
1½ tsp salt

Mix all the ingredients.
Follow the method for
meatballs on page 143.

Potatoes and aubergines in tahini cream

PAGE 47, 1½ TIMES RECIPE

Baked carrots with ras el hanout

PAGE 42, 1½ TIMES RECIPE

or

Baked carrots with cumin and honey

PAGE 38, 1½ TIMES RECIPE

Arabic inspired Caesar salad

PAGE 81, 1½ TIMES RECIPE

Pita bread

RECIPE PAGE 147

THE DAY BEFORE

Make the meatballs
Make the tahini cream
Bake the aubergines
Peel the carrots and leave
them in water
Mix the spices

ON THE DAY ITSELF

Heat the meatballs for
15 minutes at 175°C hot air/
gas 6
Make the rest

His buffet

**Roast beef silverside/
topside**
RECIPE PAGE 141

**Beef meatballs with
ham and sage**
RECIPE PAGE 143

**Potatoes with lemon
oil and horseradish**
PAGE 46, 2½ TIMES RECIPE

Italian salad our way
PAGE 37, 1½ TIMES RECIPE

**Spelt bread and
butter**
PAGE 147, ½ - 1 RECIPE

THE DAY BEFORE
Make the meatballs
Bake the carrots and pod
the peas for the Italian salad
Make the dough for the
spelt bread

ON THE DAY ITSELF
Heat the meatballs for
15 minutes at 175°C hot air/
gas 6
Make the rest

Her buffet

**Salmon tartare
with wasabi**
PAGE 133, 1 PORTION

**Salad with goat's
cheese, walnuts and
honey**
PAGE 82, 1½ PORTIONS

**Baked peppers with
rocket vinaigrette**
PAGE 94, 1½ TIMES RECIPE

**Beetroot in yoghurt
with herbs**
PAGE 19, 1½ TIMES RECIPE

Spelt bread and butter
PAGE 147, ½ - 1 TIMES RECIPE

THE DAY BEFORE
Toast the nuts for the
    mixed salads
Make the vinaigrette for
    the peppers
Boil the beetroots
Make the dough for the
    spelt bread

ON THE DAY ITSELF
Make the rest

Asian buffet#1

Asian prawn cocktail
PAGE 102, DOUBLE THE RECIPE

Chicken satay skewers with peanut sauce
RECIPE PAGE 144

Vegetable sticks
FROM 1 ½ KG
Unprepared vegetables, for example, Chinese radishes, carrots, cucumber, peppers.

Noodles with spinach and toasted cashew nuts
PAGE 54, 1 ½ TIMES RECIPE

Prawn crackers
Available from supermarkets or Chinese grocers, follow the instructions on the packet.

THE DAY BEFORE
Make the peanut sauce
Toast the cashew nuts

ON THE DAY ITSELF
Make the rest

All the smaller buffets are for 8 people

Asian buffet #2

Salmon tartare with wasabi
RECIPE PAGE 133

Thai inspired chicken salad
PAGE 105, 1½ TIMES RECIPE

Crisp vegetables in red curry cream
PAGE 29, 1½ TIMES RECIPE

Salad with seaweed and green beans
PAGE 29, DOUBLE THE RECIPE
See White fish with seaweed and green beans, leave out the fish

Prawn crackers
Available from supermarkets or Chinese grocers, follow the instructions on the packet.

EVERYTHING TO BE MADE
ON THE DAY

Indian Buffet

Indian meatballs
PAGE 143, 1½ TIMES RECIPE

Indian inspired potato salad
PAGE 50, 1½ TIMES RECIPE

Melon tzatziki
PAGE 116, 1½ TIMES RECIPE

Salad with spicy nuts
PAGE 83, 1½ TIMES RECIPE

Chapati
PAGE 147, DOUBLE THE RECIPE

or Pita bread
RECIPE PAGE 147

THE DAY BEFORE
Make the meatballs
Prepare the spicy nuts

ON THE DAY ITSELF
Heat the meatballs for 15
    minutes at 175°C hot air/
    gas 6
Make the rest

Mediterranean buffet

Salade nicoise with fresh tuna
PAGE 99, DOUBLE THE RECIPE

Meat on skewers
PAGE 144, DOUBLE THE RECIPE

Baked peppers with rocket vinaigrette
PAGE 94, 1½ TIMES RECIPE

White and green beans with anchovy mayonnaise
PAGE 64, 1½ TIMES RECIPE

Spelt bread and butter
PAGE 147, ½ - 1 TIMES RECIPE

THE DAY BEFORE
Prepare the marinade for
    the skewers
Make the vinaigrette for
    the peppers
Soak the white beans,
    trim the green beans
Make the anchovy mayonnaise
Make the dough for the
    spelt bread

ON THE DAY ITSELF
Make the rest

Party buffets

For the party buffets we have used the most neutral dishes as they are generally good to serve to a lot of people, who have many different ideas about flavours and food. In order to gather the guests round the table, it is a good idea to start with an individual portion as a first course (for example salmon tartare, prawn cocktail or a fish salad) which can be ready served on plates. Then you move on to the main course and the dessert which is laid out as a buffet.

All the party buffets are for 20 people. The four big party buffets have been composed on the basis of seasonal raw materials.

Many people don't like the buffet form of serving food. Partly because the delicious dishes end up as a mishmash on the plate and partly because they hate queuing for food. We have suggestions for both. Make an attractive menu card where you clearly indicate which salads to have first and with which meat or fish dishes they should be enjoyed. You could also put small signs at the dishes so your guests can easily find their way round the buffet. Arrange the dishes on the buffet in the order they should be enjoyed – i.e. in the same order as they are written on the menu card: Fish dishes with salad side dishes, fish salads, meat dishes with the rest of the salads, followed by cheese, bread, butter, cake or dessert.

For smaller parties you could pass the dishes round to the guests in the order they should be enjoyed and with breaks in between to digest the delicacies.

The four big party buffets have been based on the seasonal raw materials available. The dishes for the buffets can be prepared over several days so you are not completely exhausted when the guests arrive. It is a good idea to photocopy the chosen recipes, get an understanding of the workload, prepare a shopping list and work out the work strategy. Generally the dishes should not be served directly from the fridge, but should be taken out half an hour before serving.

Also remember to dress salads and any garnish only at the last minute before serving.

Alternatively you can make the buffets less work intensive if you ask your guests to bring a dish each and then you provide the drinks.

Spring buffet

	THE DAY BEFORE	ON THE DAY ITSELF
Romaine salad with, croutons, lumpfish roe and avocado cream PAGE 10, 3½ TIMES RECIPE Can be served as a first course arranged on individual plates	Wash the romaine lettuce and leave in plastic bags. Make the croutons and cover them lightly	Make the rest
Fish on skewers PAGE 139, DOUBLE THE RECIPE	Make the tapenade for the asparagus	
Asparagus with spinach, egg and tapenade PAGE 87, 3½ TIMES RECIPE		Make the rest
Roast leg of lamb PAGE 141, DOUBLE THE RECIPE		Roast the leg of lamb
Beef meatballs with ham and sage PAGE 143, DOUBLE THE RECIPE	Make the meatballs	Heat the meatballs in the oven for 15 minutes at 200°C hot air/gas 7
Baked potatoes with lemons and herbs PAGE 47, 4 TIMES RECIPE	Scrub the potatoes and leave them in water	Make the rest
Tina's tzatziki PAGE 116, 4 TIMES RECIPE		Make the salad
Cheeses of your choice 1 KG IN TOTAL		Arrange the cheeses
Spelt bread and butter PAGE 147, DOUBLE THE RECIPE AND 200 G BUTTER	Make the dough for the spelt bread	Bake the bread
Rhubarb cake with ginger PAGE 150, DOUBLE THE RECIPE	Make the rhubarb compote	Make the cake

Summer buffet
SEE PHOTO PAGE 130-1

The lines indicate which dishes should be placed together on the buffet and served together. The first course can be arranged as individual portions.

	THE DAY BEFORE	ON THE DAY ITSELF
Salmon tartare with herbs PAGE 135, 3 TIMES RECIPE Serve as a first course with a green salad and bread		Make the rest
Carpaccio of fillet of beef RECIPE PAGE 142	Brown the meat for the carpaccio and put it in the freezer	Make the rest
Tomatoes with fried peppers and mozzarella PAGE 90, 3½ TIMES RECIPE		Make the salad
Meat on skewers PAGE 144, DOUBLE THE RECIPE	Marinade the meat and put it on skewers	Make the rest
Potatoes with rocket and pine kernels PAGE 50, 4 TIMES RECIPE	Scrub the potatoes and leave them in water. Toast the pine kernels, wash the rocket and make the dressing for the potatoes	Make the salad
Salad with strawberries and elderflower PAGE 84, 3½ TIMES RECIPE, LEAVE OUT THE PINE KERNELS	Wash the iceberg lettuce, make the dressing	Make the salad
Pea and mint tzatziki PAGE 116, 4 TIMES RECIPE	Pod the peas for the tzatziki	Make the salad
Cheeses 1 KG IN TOTAL		Arrange the cheeses
Spelt bread and butter PAGE 147, DOUBLE THE RECIPE AND 200 G BUTTER	Make the dough for the spelt bread	Bake the bread
Meringue cake with whipped cream, redcurrant and white chocolate PAGE 148, DOUBLE THE RECIPE	Bake the meringues, garnish with the chocolate	Make the cake

Winter buffet
SEE PAGE 167

BEEF MEATBALLS WITH HAM AND THYME

MIXED GREEN SALAD WITH BALSA-
MIC VINEGAR DRESSING

PASTA SALAD WITH MUSHROOMS,
CRANBERRIES AND HAZELNUTS

CHOCOLATE MOUSSE WITH FRUIT
IN MUSCOVADO SYRUP

BAKED POTATOES
WITH LEMON

AVOCADO CREAM

CHEESES

SPELT BREAD

SALMON TARTARE WITH WASABI

FRIED DUCK BREAST

Autumn buffet

Salad with goat's cheese, walnuts and honey

PAGE 82, 3½ TIMES RECIPE

Can be served in individual portions as a first course with bread

	THE DAY BEFORE	ON THE DAY ITSELF
	Toast the walnuts, make the dressing and wash the salad	Make the rest Arrange the salad

Whole oven baked salmon

RECIPE PAGE 134

		Bake the fish

Potatoes and beetroot in horseradish cream

PAGE 45, 4 TIMES RECIPE

	Peel and boil the beetroot, make the horseradish cream	Make the rest

Meatballs with cranberries and pistachio nuts

PAGE 143, 3 TIMES RECIPE

	Make the meatballs	Heat the meatballs in the oven for 15 minutes at 200°C hot air/gas 7

Baked root vegetables with thyme

PAGE 43, 3½ TIMES RECIPE

Leave out garlic mayonnaise and use 1½ tbsp balsamic vinegar per recipe

	Peel the root vegetables and put them in water with a little lemon juice	Make the rest

Roast beef topside/silverside

PAGE 141, DOUBLE THE RECIPE

		Roast the meat

Coleslaw

Cut 1 kg white cabbage finely, grate 500 g carrots coarsely, mix with a cream of 600 g Greek yoghurt 10%, 1 tbsp Dijon mustard, 1 tbsp sugar, 1 tbsp lemon juice and 1 tbsp finely grated onion. Season to taste with salt and pepper.

	Make the cream for the coleslaw	Make the salad

Cheeses

1 KG IN TOTAL

		Arrange the cheeses

Spelt bread and butter

PAGE 147, DOUBLE THE RECIPE AND 200 G BUTTER

	Make the dough for the spelt bread	Bake the bread

Apple trifle

PAGE 150, DOUBLE THE RECIPE

	Make the apple sauce and breadcrumbs	Make the cake

Winter buffet SEE PHOTO PAGE 164-165

	THE DAY BEFORE	ON THE DAY ITSELF
Salmon tartare with wasabi PAGE 133, 3 TIMES RECIPE Can be served as a first course with a green salad and bread		Make the salmon tartare
Beef meatballs with ham and thyme SEE BEEF MEATBALLS WITH HAM AND SAGE, PAGE 143 3 TIMES RECIPE Replace sage with thyme	Make the meatballs	Heat the meatballs for 15 minutes at 175°C hot air/ gas 6
Baked potatoes with lemon and herbs PAGE 47, 4 TIMES RECIPE	Scrub/peel the potatoes and leave them in water	Make the rest
Avocado cream Mash 8 ripe avocadoes, mix with 2 crushed garlic cloves, 2 tbsp lemon juice, 1.2 kg crème fraîche 9% fat, salt and pepper		Make the cream
Fried duck breast PAGE 141, DOUBLE THE RECIPE		Fry the duck breasts
Pasta with mushrooms, cranberries and hazelnuts PAGE 62, 3½ TIMES RECIPE	Toast the hazelnuts	Make the salad
Mixed green salad with balsamic vinegar dressing 1.5 kg green salads of your choice in mouth-size pieces, dressing of 100 ml olive oil, 2 tbsp balsamic vinegar, 1½ tsp sugar, salt and pepper	Wash the iceberg salad, make the dressing	Make the rest
Cheeses 1 KG IN TOTAL		Arrange the cheeses
Spelt bread and butter PAGE 147, DOUBLE THE RECIPE AND 200 G BUTTER	Make the dough for the spelt bread	Bake the bread
Chocolate mousse with fruit in muscovado syrup PAGE 153, DOUBLE THE RECIPE	Make the chocolate mousse and syrup	Arrange the dessert

Superb seasons

We should use local vegetables and fruit when they are in season:

• They have the best flavour because they are super fresh and naturally ripened.

• They have not been transported from the other side of the world – that may damage the environment.

• Seasonal fruit and vegetables provide a good variation for the meals throughout the year, so you do not end up eating tomatoes, cucumber or broccoli every day.

• The variation helps to cover your nutritional needs.

• Vegetables in season are often cheaper.

Use the seasonal chart when you are planning your menu Make dishes from the raw materials that are either in high season or season. When you have found the vegetables and fruits that are in season on the chart, you look up the index on page 170 to find the dishes containing these raw materials. You can also find all our recipes via the raw materials on: www.salathovederne.dk

Season for local fruit, berries and nuts from open ground

■ ■ ■ ■ = SEASON ▬▬▬ HIGH SEASON

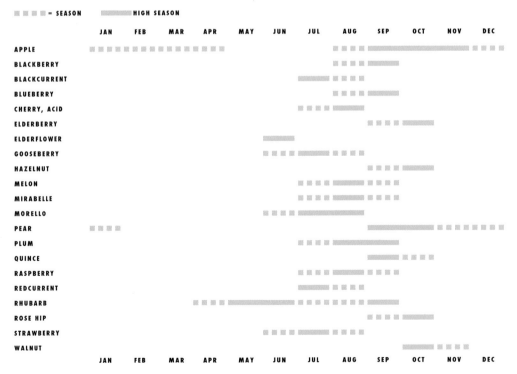

	JAN	FEB	MAR	APR	MAY	JUN	JUL	AUG	SEP	OCT	NOV	DEC
APPLE	S	S	S	S	S			S	H	H	H	S
BLACKBERRY								S	H			
BLACKCURRENT							H	S				
BLUEBERRY								S	H			
CHERRY, ACID							S	S				
ELDERBERRY									S	H		
ELDERFLOWER						H						
GOOSEBERRY						S	S	H				
HAZELNUT									S	H		
MELON							S	S	H			
MIRABELLE							S	S	H			
MORELLO						S	S	S				
PEAR	S	S							H	H	H	S
PLUM							S	H				
QUINCE									H	S		
RASPBERRY							S	H				
REDCURRENT							H	S				
RHUBARB				S	H	H	S	S				
ROSE HIP									S	H		
STRAWBERRY					S	S	S	S				
WALNUT										H	S	

| | JAN | FEB | MAR | APR | MAY | JUN | JUL | AUG | SEP | OCT | NOV | DEC |

Season for local vegetables from open ground and glasshouses

▪ ▪ ▪ ▪ = SEASON   ▒▒▒▒ HIGH SEASON

	JAN	FEB	MAR	APR	MAY	JUN	JUL	AUG	SEP	OCT	NOV	DEC
ASPARAGUS												
AUBERGINE												
BABY LEAVES												
BEANS												
BEETROOT												
-NEW												
BROCCOLI												
BRUSSELS SPROUTS												
CARROT												
-NEW												
CAULIFLOWER												
CELERIAC												
CELERY												
CHERRY TOMATO												
CUCUMBER												
-PICKLING												
ENDIVE												
FENNEL												
GREEN CABBAGE												
HAMBURG PARSLEY												
HORSERADISH												
JERUSALEM ARTICHOKES												
LEEK												
LETTUCE												
MUSHROOMS												
MUSHROOMS, WILD												
ONION												
-NEW												
PARSNIP												
PEAS												
PEPPER												
POINTED CABBAGE												
POTATOES												
PUMPKIN, EDIBLE												
RADISH												
RED CABBAGE												
SAVOY CABBAGE												
SCORZONERA												
SPINACH												
SPRING ONION												
SQUASH												
SUMMER WHITE CABBAGE												
SWEET CORN												
TOMATO												
TURNIP												
WHITE CABBAGE												

	JAN	FEB	MAR	APR	MAY	JUN	JUL	AUG	SEP	OCT	NOV	DEC

Index

A

Anchovy mayonnaise 64
Apple trifle 150
Arabic buffet 155
Arabic inspired Caesar salad 81
Arabic meatballs 155
Arabic slaw 30
Asian buffet 158, 159
Asian green cabbage salad 27
Asian prawn cocktail 102
Asparagus with egg, spinach & tapenade 87
Asparagus, baked with Parma ham 87
Aubergine in tahini cream 47
Aubergine, baked 97
Aubergines, fried 94
Autumn buffet 166
Avocado & bean salsa 114
Avocado & lime salsa 123
Avocado cream 100, 167
Avocado salad with tomato, oregano & feta cheese 97
Avocado tzatziki 116
Avocado with rhubarb compote 97
Avocado, sweetcorn & tomato salsa 123

B

Baked asparagus with Parma ham 87
Baked aubergines with yoghurt 97
Baked beetroot with caraway seed & yoghurt 23
Baked beetroot with crunchy salsa verde 23
Baked carrots with 3 kinds of seed 38
Baked carrots with cumin & honey 38
Baked carrots with ras el hanout 42
Baked carrots with seeds 38
Baked celeriac with gremolata 43
Baked celeriac with tapenade 42
Baked Hamburg parsley with clementines & linseed 38
Baked peppers 94
Baked potatoes with herbs & lemon 47
Baked pumpkin with tarragon 92

Baked root vegetables with garlic mayonnaise 43
Baked root vegetables with poppy seeds 43
Balsamic dressing 129
Balsamic vinegar 11
Basil cream 106
Basmati rice 12
Beans & rice salad 68
Beans with mint hazelnut pesto 67
Beans, 64, 65, 67, 103, 114
Beef 141, 142, 143
Beef meat balls with ham & sage 143
Beetroot in yoghurt with herbs 19
Beetroot salad with beetroot bruschetta 20
Beetroot salads 18, 19, 20, 22, 23, 30, 45
Beetroot with crunchy salsa verde 18, 23
Beetroot with dill & lemon zest 22
Beetroot with yoghurt, coffee & walnuts 18, 23
Brunch buffet 155
Brunch salad 111
Bruschetta 20
Brussels sprouts with clementines & dates & nut mint salsa 32
Brussels sprouts with pistachio nuts 34
Brussels sprouts with red salad onion & feta cheese 34
Buckwheat noodles 12
Buckwheat noodles with crisp vegetables & peanut cream 56
Buffets 155-167
Bulgur salad with chicken 105
Bulgur with aubergines 58
Bulgur with courgettes 58
Bulgur with herbs 59

C

Cabbage, 24, 27, 28, 29, 30, 31, 34
Cabbage salad with seaweed & sesame oil 29
Caesar salad, 81
Carpaccio of fillet of beef 142
Carrots 37, 38, 42, 43
Celeriac 42, 43
Celeriac skordalia 119
Ceviche à la Japan 138
Ceviche with pomegranate 138
Chapatti 147
Cherry tomatoes & Jerusalem artichokes in peanut cream 90
Chicken salad with aubergine 106

Chicken salad, Thai inspired 105
Chicken satay with peanut sauce 144
Chicken with bulgur salad 105
Chicken, spinach & lentils in curry cream 105
Chinese inspired duck breast salad 106
Chinese sweet & sour dressing 126
Chocolate mousse 153
Coconut flakes 12
Coffee cream 23
Coleslaw 31, 166
Courgette, bulgur with 58
Cranberries 40
Creamy lemon dressing 127
Crisp vegetables in curry cream 29
Croutons, 81, 100
Crunchy Thai salsa 118
Cucumber & mango with Parma ham 112
Curry cream 29

D

Dill, beetroot salad with 22
Duck 34, 106, 141

E

Edamame beans 12, 70
Elderflower dressing 84
Elderflower, salads with 84
Energy bomb salad 70

F

Fennel with oranges 111
Feta 13, 40, 97, 112
Fish buffets 132
Fish salad in spicy sauce 100
Fish skewers 139
Fish tartare with dill & Dijon mustard 135
Fish tartare with lime & coriander 135
Fish with green beans 103
Fried aubergines & radishes with miso dressing 94
Fried peppers with mozzarella 90
Fruit in muscovado syrup 153

G

Garlic 17
Garlic mayonnaise 43
Goat's cheese 82

Goat's cheese cream 54
Granny's dressing with variations 80
Grapefruit, brunch salad with 111
Green beans with mint hazelnut pesto 67
Green olive & almond tapenade 122
Green salad with Hamburg parsley chips 79
Gremolata 43

H

Hamburg parsley 38, 43, 79
Herbs, fresh 17, 19
Horseradish cream 45, 89, 128
Hummus, spinach 121

I

Iceberg salad with cherries 81
Indian buffet 159
Indian inspired potato salad 50
Indian meatballs 143
Italian inspired tomato & bread salad 89
Italian salad 37

J

Jerusalem artichokes in peanut cream 90

L

Lamb 141
Lamb shank with garam masala 142
Lavender whipped cream 151
Lemon dressing 50, 127
Lemon pine kernel cake 151
Lime leaves 13
Lumpfish roe 100

M

Mango with Parma ham 112
Mayonnaise 43, 64
Meat skewers 144
Meatballs with cranberries 143
Melon tzatziki 116
Meringue cake 148
Mexi slaw 28
Mexican inspired Caesar salad 81
Mint hazelnut pesto 67
Miso 11
Miso dressing 48, 94, 127

Mushrooms 59, 61
Mussels, pasta with 99
Mussels, steamed in white wine 133
Mustard dressing with herbs 126

N

Noodles with beans & peanuts 55
Noodles with oyster mushrooms 59
Noodles with spinach 56
Nut mint salsa 32
Nuts, spicy 83

O

Olive oil 11
Olive oil balsamic vinegar dressing 129
Orange salad with red salad onion & mint 111
Orange salad with tandoori spice 109
Oranges with fennel 111
Oranges with olives & cream 110

P

Pasta 17
Pasta with grilled lemon 54
Pasta with mushrooms 54
Pasta with mussels & saffron 99
Pasta with slow cooked tomatoes & goat's cheese cream 54
Pasta with slow cooked tomatoes 52
Pea & mint tzatziki 116
Pea cream 37
Peanut butter 11
Peanut cream 56, 90, 128
Peanut sauce 144
Peperonata cream 122
Pepper 11
Pepper, red & feta dip 122
Peppers 94, 122
Pesto 67, 129
Pita bread 147
Pomegranate, with ceviche 138
Potato salad with mushrooms, spinach & miso dressing 48
Potato salad with Nigella seeds 50
Potatoes & aubergines 47
Potatoes & beetroot in horseradish cream 45
Potatoes & olives 47
Potatoes in spring 46

Potatoes with horseradish & lemon oil 46
Potatoes with rocket 50
Potatoes with zhug 46
Prawn cocktail 102, 103
Pumpkin, baked 92

Q

Quinoa 11
Quinoa-tabbouleh 62

R

Ras el hanout 42
Raspberry vinaigrette 126
Red cabbage slaw with beetroot & tarragon cream 30
Red cabbage with fruit & toasted walnuts 24
Red curry cream 29
Rhubarb compote 97
Rhubarb cream 46
Rhubarb layer cake 150
Rice & bean salad 68
Rice noodles & prawns in sweet & sour sauce 58
Rocket vinaigrette 94
Romaine salad with lumpfish roe 100

S

Salad à la Christmas Eve 34
Salad with goat's cheese & honey 82
Salad with spicy nuts 83
Salade niçoise with fresh tuna 99
Salads, general 17
Salads with strawberries & elderflowers 84
Salmon baked 134
Salmon tartare with herbs 135
Salmon tartare with wasabi 133
Salsa verde 23
Salsas, 32, 114, 118, 123
Satay sauce 139
Sautéed summer turnip with cranberries & feta 40
Seaweed 12, 29, 70, 103, 138
Sesame oil 11, 29
Sesame omelette 59
Sesame seed oil dressing 29
Skordalia, celeriac 119
Slow baked tomatoes 52, 54
Sonja's favourite salad 67
Soy sauce 12
Spelt 12
Spelt bread 147

Spelt salad with fried plums, mushrooms & rosemary 61
Spices, ground 11
Spicy nuts 83
Spinach & avocado tzatziki 116
Spinach 87
Spinach hummus 121
Spinach, lentils & chicken in curry cream 105
Spring buffet 162
Spring slaw 31
Spring tzatziki 116
Strawberries, salads with 84
Sugar 13
Summer buffet 163
Summer slaw 28
Sweet & sour dressing 126
Sweet & sour sauce 58
Sweetcorn cream 89
Sweetcorn, avocado & tomato salsa 79

T

Tabbouleh 62
Tahini cream 47
Tahini dressing 128
Tahini sauce 139
Tapenade 42, 87, 122
Tarragon cream 30
Techniques 14, 15
Thai inspired chicken salad 105
Thousand Island dressing 129
Thyme & garlic mayonnaise 43
Tina's tzatziki 116
Tomato salad à la Mexico 89
Tomatoes with horseradish cream 89
Tomatoes with peppers & mozzarella 90
Tomatoes with 3 kinds of cheese 88
Tuna, salade niçoise with 99
Turkey breast roast with herbs 142
Turnip, summer 40
Tzatziki 116

V

Veal 141
Vinaigrette, 94, 126

W

Walnuts 23, 24, 58, 82, 97
Wasabi 12, 70, 127, 133
Watermelon with feta 112
White & green beans with anchovy mayonnaise 64
White fish tartare with dill & Dijon mustard 135
White fish tartare with lime & coriander 135
White fish with seaweed & green beans 103
Winter buffet 167

Y

Yoghurt 13, 19, 23, 97
Yoghurt dressing 28, 128

Z

Zest, 14
Zhug 46

3 superb salad sisters

SONJA BOCK

Salad Sonja

Cook book writer. Gives talks and workshops to work place kitchens, among others. Consultant dietician to small and large kitchens. Cooks for parties.

Worked in catering and has for many years helped to make lunches and party buffets exciting, delicious tasting and full of vitamins. Worked in the kitchen in Flora's Coffee bar and together with Tina created the Superb Salads Concept.

Born 1964 and trained as a kitchen manager.

My relationship with salads: 'I never eat a meal without and I believe it is the best and easiest way of having vegetables every day. My meals are always based on the salads rather than the meat or fish. My son too doesn't like a meal without salads!'

MAIL@SALATSONJA.DK

TINA SCHEFTELOWITZ

The salad head

Food writer, cook book writer, product/ and concept developer, entrepreneur.

Mother of Flora's Coffee bar and Amokka, develops healthy fast food for supermarkets, consultant for cafes and restaurants, lectures and runs courses, food writer for the Monthly magazine IN and Politiken. Has written 10 cook books. Through voluntary work has supported among others the Danish Red Cross and Danish Refugee Council.

Born 1964 and trained as a kitchen manager.

My relationship with salads: 'It is a way of life…..'

WWW.SALATHOVEDERNE.DK

ALETTE BERTELSEN

Graphic designer. Works with book design, packaging, ideas and visual identity.
Born 1973 and trained as a graphic designer.
My relationship with salads: 'Sonja and Tina have taught me to cook, just as I design: To play with colours and flavours – what do I have in the cupboard and what can I do with it? And voila – I have a fantastic meal. It is fun!'

WWW.IMPERIET.DK

PHOTOS BY DITTE ISAGER, COLUMBUS LETH AND ANDERS SCHØNNEMANN